SOCIAL
SPEECHES

SOCIAL SPEECHES

by

**Gordon Williams
& Andrew Armitage**

With 622 jokes and quotations compiled by
Kevin Goldstein-Jackson
G F Lamb
A C H Newman

Contents

Introduction

Making a social speech is about more than just standing up and 'saying a few words'. There are some who can do this without worrying, and we gape in admiration at the seeming ease with which they stand before an assembly of expectant guests, both known and unknown, and release a riot of *bons mots* that glitter in their gushing profusion.

This is not to say, however, that the task need be a daunting one. Preparation is the key (yes, even for 'impromptu' speeches), and this book will go a long way in preparing *you* for the task.

Not only does it bring together a number of ready-made social speeches for almost every conceivable occasion, but it also gives you added material with which to modify those speeches to suit your own temperament and the prevailing circumstances.

By far the commonest occasion at which people find themselves called upon to speak is a wedding, and many of the ready-made speeches in this book are wedding speeches of one sort or another, and among them you will find tips and comments on wedding-reception protocol.

But there are also speeches for introducing visiting speakers, welcoming foreign guests, opening special events, making appeals and many other purposes. And it takes little imagination to extract ideas from one speech to use in another, which may be for a very different purpose.

Look upon this book as a workshop: an array of components for customising your speech, and tools in the form of tips along the way, helping you to assemble the components into a polished whole.

I will change the metaphor and say let nothing be set in stone, but allow your imagination to remould the thing as the necessity arises.

On the other hand, there may be speeches in these pages that are almost perfect for the occasion, just as they are.

The speeches and much of the linking material have been written by the late Gordon Williams, himself a public speaker of note, who actually delivered some of the speeches printed here during his years in public life. The quotations have been largely assembled by Geoffrey Lamb and most of the jokes written by Kevin Goldstein-Jackson.

For my own part, I have brought together material in a way I hope will be useful and accessible – and, of course, lively and interesting. I have added linking material where I felt it would help the reader, and have supplied tips and material on how to use the book to the best advantage.

I hope you will enjoy reading and using this cornucopia of speech materials as much as I have enjoyed the task of editing it.

Andrew Armitage, LGSM

Part 1
The Preparation

1

How To Get The Best
From This Book

Most books – even practical ones – are best read from beginning to end, with practice exercises, where appropriate, performed along the route. This is not one of them.

However, if you *wish* to read it through from the first page to the last you will still get a lot of enjoyment and instruction from it. But you could as usefully start in the middle and move in either direction – and to some extent this is what you may find yourself doing.

There are two important indexes within this book: one at the end of the *Quotations* section and one at the end of the *Jokes* section. The entries in these indexes do more than merely refer you to a thing or person; they also guide you to concepts and ideas. For instance, you may find the entry *Innocence* leading you to the same joke or quotation as *Children;* and *Sod's Law* could take you in the same direction as *Frustration* or one of a number of other entries.

In many instances you won't find the words *Frustration, Children* and *Sod's Law* there in the anecdote or quotation itself – but you *will* find a situation depicted that reflects the index entry that led you there.

So these two indexes would be a good place to begin. Familiarise yourself with them, and the ideas within them. Just as you would know where all the tools were in your workshop or utensils in your kitchen, so you can begin to categorise, sort and pigeon-hole the ideas in the indexes according to the way they will work best for you.

A weaving of threads
Just as individual threads and colours woven into a garment are indistinguishable from the garment as a whole, components of a speech should be an integral part of the speech and not look like an extra bit of material that has been tacked on as an afterthought. In the speeches themselves, you will find plenty of examples of this weaving of threads, as a story or joke is introduced as a digression before the speech gently resumes its course. To do otherwise would create an artificial and jerky speech with the joins showing.

So briefly study the way it is done and use those ideas to weave in a joke or quotation of your choice – whether it is from this book or from your own imagination or another source.

These digressions spice up a speech or add a little leaven to punctuate the more serious points you wish to make. As such, they should be as appropriate as you can make them. A simple clause such as '...I'm reminded of another gathering similar to this one, where I met a man who...' is adequate to weave your anecdote into a speech. Don't worry too much if the digression doesn't add to the accumulated wisdom of your audience, but, if it serves to hammer home a point *and* is amusing, then all the better.

Preparing for the 'impromptu' speech
Have you ever been frustratedly envious of those people who seem to have words ready for any occasion? If you are in a social position whereby you could well be asked to stand and say a few words, and if your memory is good, you could usefully put together several cores of speeches and have them in a mental note form in your brain. When you have to do the deed, it should not be too difficult to 'top and tail' the core with a few words appropriate to the occasion.

This sort of challenge is more likely to arise in an informal situation rather than a wedding or dinner, so don't worry if what you eventually say is a little rough around the edges. That will soon be forgotten in the

12

admiration of your listeners for the seemingly off-the-cuff but incredibly apt remarks that are still ringing in their appreciative ears.

Protocol
You will need to use accepted forms of address on more formal occasions. Even if you don't believe in that sort of thing and consider it pompous, to ignore it could invite ridicule because, unless you explain your reasons for ignoring the accepted form, your audience will just think you ignorant. And if you *do* explain your reasons your allotted time will be up before you get to the meat of your speech!

If ever you should address a monarch, begin with 'Your Majesty, Mr [or Madam] Chairman...', as you would if you were addressing the Queen Mother. The Duke of Edinburgh: 'May it please Your Royal Highness, Mr [or Madam] Chairman...' etc. The Prince of Wales would be treated in the same way, as would the Princess Royal and immediate members of the Royal Family.

If a Prime Minister is in your audience, say 'Mr [or Madam] Prime Minister'. If a knight is guest of honour, you would begin with 'Sir'. A duke would receive 'My Lord Duke' or 'Your Grace'; a marquess, 'My Lord Marquess'; a baron, earl or viscount, 'My Lord'.

For an archbishop, say 'Your Grace'; a bishop, 'My Lord'.

You would address an ambassador as 'Your Excellency'.

A city has a lord mayor and a town a mayor. They should be addressed as 'My Lord Mayor' and 'Your Worship' respectively – even if the holder of the office is a woman. Sexist it may be, but that's the way it is. A female lord mayor is not to be confused with a lady mayoress, by the way; the latter is the female consort of the lord mayor, and should be addressed as 'Lady Mayoress'.

Structuring your speech
You will ultimately find a way to use this book that suits you. But one method that may prove useful to begin with

is to copy out the speech you're going to deliver, stopping at the points where jokes or quotations are, and ask if another might be more appropriate to your purposes (see *Personalising* below). Find it and weave it into the body of your speech and then get back on course with a smooth transition that leaves your listeners believing that your choice of quotation or anecdote was the definitive one, and could not possibly have merely been dropped in.

Personalising

Often you can personalise a story by using someone in the room as the person referred to. But this will have to be an occasion when such an artifice will be taken in good spirit. If you're the best man at a wedding, for instance, and you know the bridegroom very well, he is not going to mind some friendly leg-pulling, even if the 'true' story in which he features has come as a complete surprise to him.

Anyway, *facts* as such are not always the path to an ultimate truth. George Bernard Shaw said, 'To tell the truth is to tell the best jokes in the world'.

So this is one occasion when you can tell a pack of lies and not be believed – yet be applauded for it.

On best behaviour

It is difficult to refuse a drink at a wedding reception, but if you are going to be making a speech do be careful. It is easier, perhaps, to say no at a more formal dinner, as the host will be aware of the task that awaits you once the eating is done. And certain occasions will have no drink present to tempt you.

Do, though, be wary of yielding to the temptation to take too much to drink at an informal occasion, when spirits are probably high and people are in party mood. A small one to calm nerves is one thing; being legless is quite another, and you will not be able to deliver your speech and will become a laughing stock. Be warned!

But be consoled, too, because there's usually plenty of time for drinks once the speeches are over – as long as you are among friends. With more formal occasions to which you have been invited as a guest speaker, it is better to keep the drink to a minimum – even after the speeches. It may be frustrating but this is better by far than carrying with you the dubious reputation of being the idiot who led the conga around the tables and headbutted the archbishop because he refused to join in.

Body and soul – and visual aids

Sound enthusiastic at all times, and don't be afraid to use body language. Gesture mingles with speech to help to form and add soul to the entire ensemble of communication we refer to as a speech or talk. But don't overdo the gestures – let them remain in keeping with the occasion.

As for notes, don't be afraid to let them be seen. No one expects you to deliver a speech without any form of prompt. If you are planning to read verbatim from a pre-written speech, think again. Do it only if you can make your speech sound spontaneous. Try your delivery out on someone first and ask how you come over. If you can practise your speech from notes, then refine and polish the notes as you rehearse and rehearse, so much the better.

If you intend to use visual aids such as an overhead projector, slide projector, video, whiteboard or flipchart, make sure everything is as it should be. Check your slides; check that you've brought along the correct video tape and not the one you shot during last year's holiday on the nudist beach. Do you have some spare whiteboard markers and a duster? Many's the time a speaker has had to pull out a grubby handkerchief when no whiteboard duster has been available. Are there enough empty pages in your flipchart, or, indeed, the right pre-prepared ones?

It's always best to check with the organisers of a meeting you've been asked to address to find out what is available – and that goes for the PA system too. If you get a chance, try it out an hour or two before your 'performance'. If you *are* using a microphone, don't try to eat it. You'll have the room full of popping or screeching with feedback.

If you can inject something topical into your speech –

perhaps by amending one of the jokes or anecdotes in this collection – then do so. It makes a speech taken from a book, or one that's been dusted off a few times, sound so much fresher and more spontaneous. Keep an eye and ear to the news for a few days before your speech.

Dress for the occasion. A dapper suit or evening dress isn't required garb for addressing a political rally outside a factory. On the other hand, you should wear more formal dress for a dinner engagement, and find out beforehand whether the requirement is for evening dress or lounge suits. It is better on these occasions to adhere to the 'when in Rome' maxim, and do as the Romans do.

There are a thousand and one possible tips, but those above are among the cardinal ones. A final one concerns your voice. You'll get its measure as you practise your speech during the days before the occasion. Again, try it out on a listener. Don't shout. Learn to project by good posture, pushing gently from the diaphragm and addressing the back of the hall. Use clear consonants and well-rounded vowels, because the very shapes of words can get lost in acoustically unsuitable buildings or in the open air.

Perhaps the best tip of all is to enjoy yourself. If you enjoy the process of gathering materials, assembling them and delivering them to an appreciative audience, much of the above should follow automatically.

2
Constructing a Social Speech

Every social or other speech requires three separate parts: a beginning, a middle and an end. In other words, introduction, development and conclusion.

The beginning should capture the attention of the audience and introduce the subject. The middle is its development or exposition. Here the audience is told what you want it to know and how it is affected. Speak brightly, no matter what the occasion. The end is not just a finishing or trailing off: rather, it should be a well-considered rounding off, which leaves the audience feeling satisfied with a speech to be remembered.

On social occasions we don't normally lecture, preach or explain. Sometimes we congratulate, but usually we welcome guests or say thank you for the hospitality.

It would be easy if we could just congratulate, welcome or thank people, adding a word on the future. But tradition demands that we devote long moments to saying these things, and that's where the agony may come in – especially for the audience!

Let us study the matter.

The beginning
Aim to hook your audience. This is easy when you begin your career because, if you're an unknown and inexperienced speaker, your audience will be agog with interest. This, fortunately, lasts until it becomes known that you are competent. After that you'll have to work on your audience like a professional entertainer.

The novice or unknown speaker is safe in starting speeches with thanks to the organisation for their invitation and hospitality.

When you are known, you will have to employ the

professional's devices for capturing your audience. Four of these are now described.

1. Ask a question

Start by asking your audience a question, which must, of course, be relevant to your subject or to them. You could begin a speech at a social club thus: 'Can any of you tell me what happiness is?' Then pause a moment, to let your question sink in and to allow your audience to collect their thoughts. Next, you could continue, 'Of course, many of you can tell me what happiness is. The happy looks on your faces assure me of this. Finding words to express happiness is something one might find a little difficult, though. I read recently that happiness is being satisfied with what you have got as well as with what you haven't got. A friend of mine put it this way: "Happiness is a wayside station between those two great termini, Too Little and Too Much."

'This club of yours seems to me to have a great deal to do with keeping open that wayside station...' and so on.

A variation of this beginning is to get your audience to ask questions of themselves. For instance, 'This audience has got something one does not always come across at gatherings such as this. Standing here, I can both feel and see it. *Feel* it, because every public speaker forms a bond with the audience he or she is addressing. *See* it because it's written on your faces...! What *is* this I feel and see? It's your happiness...' and so on.

2. Start with a quotation

Imagine you are addressing a tennis club. Start by saying, 'Birds of a feather flock together.' Before you're halfway through, your audience will be quoting with you willy-nilly. You will have caught their attention. Their thoughts are now focused on you and what you have to say. Pause a moment or two after your quotation and then go on to make it an integral part of your speech

For instance, 'Birds of a feather flock together. When I was at school I frequently heard this proverb quoted. But never in a complimentary sense. Always it was after two or more of us had been misbehaving. By now I have had experience enough of life to realise that my mentors did not know everything, and that this proverb can be used to describe all kinds of organisation.

'What are we here tonight but birds of a feather? The "feather" common to us is a devotion to tennis. In the fourteenth century it was known as the Game of Kings. Charles V of France actually forbade his subjects to play it...' and so forth.

3. Say something that is a complete denial of the views you are known to hold

The audience get such a surprise at hearing you uttering such a heresy that they're shocked into listening. For example, supposing you were addressing a golf club, start with, 'Golf is a good walk spoilt...!' Pause a moment to let what you have said sink in, then add, 'So said that great American author Mark Twain...' Now carry on with the body of your speech.

4. Tell a relevant story

This should not be a funny story because the art of getting a laugh out of an audience within a moment of starting a speech is most difficult. Even professional comedians find it hard to get their first laugh. It has something to do with an audience needing to warm up. Suppose you were addressing a motoring organisation...

'Recently a remarkable bus driver retired. In all the years he'd been employed by the bus company he'd never been involved in an accident. His colleagues agreed to give him a farewell party and the bus company decided that their manager should present him with a specially struck gold medal and a mantelpiece clock.

'On the night of the party the manager referred in glowing terms to the driver's record and presented him with his awards.

'Presently the driver had to reply. He did so in words something like these: "I'm no great shakes at making speeches but I suppose you all want to know how I managed all these years without an accident. Well, it's like this. There's only one way to do it. Drive as if everyone else on the road were plumb crazy!"

'Undoubtedly that is splendid advice. If everyone followed it, then the roads would be much safer places. I hope everyone in this organisation takes it to heart...' and so forth.

Aesop's fables provide a source for anecdotes of this kind. Assume you are addressing a function.

'One of Aesop's fables tells the story of a big dog and a donkey which set off on a long journey'.

'The donkey had a heavy load of bread on his back, and stopped after a while to eat grass from the hedgerow.

' "I'm hungry too," complained the dog. "Please give me a piece of bread."

' "I'm sorry," replied the donkey coldly. "I can't spare any of it. If you want to eat you must do like me – find something by the wayside."

'And so the poor dog had to do without any food.

'They walked on until presently they espied a wolf in the distance. At once the donkey began to tremble. "You're not going to run away are you, Dog?" he whined. "You'll stay and help me, won't you?"

' "I'm sorry," said the dog, "but those who eat alone will have to fight alone. Goodbye." And he left the greedy donkey to fend for himself.

'Well, you in this club are not like that donkey. You have long ago discovered that the secret of friendship, companionship and co-operation is to be friendly, companionable and co-operative. It is *because* you realise this that you are members of this club...' and so on.

The middle
If we were concerned with a speech other than a social speech, this would be the longest section. We would show how to expound your theme and put across your message. This would be where you lectured, preached or explained.

You would be told to find suitable sub-headings. You would be shown how to deal with these one by one, and how to illustrate each in turn by quotations, personal experiences, anecdotes or stories, all helping to fix points in the minds of your listeners.

You would be told to demonstrate, as you dealt with them, how each of your sub-headings affected your audience.

We are, however, concerned with *social* speeches and all you usually do in these is congratulate, welcome or thank; doing so as interestingly as possible, using anecdotes and amusing stories to enliven what you say.

Appropriate new stories are invaluable. Therefore, when you happen to come across one, record it. You will find several in this book, either among the sample speeches themselves or in the special sections devoted to anecdotes, jokes and quotations. But jot down also those you come across in other sources. You never know when it will illuminate one of your speeches.

Because it lessens the difficulty in indexing, you could record them in a loose-leaf memo book, adding pages to each section as required. A card-index box and a stack of cards are also a good idea for indexing your material. If a story is too long to record, merely jot down its source, assuming you can gain easy access to the source when you come to need it.

Some page-a-day calendars contain a thought for each day. Try to acquire one and add the aphorisms and stories that appeal to you to your own collection.

No story or joke is appropriate to every occasion. Care and ingenuity are often needed in thinking up ways of introducing them so that they don't sound out of place but form an integral part of your speech.

In this, the middle part of your speech, include words of praise for the organisation whose function you are attending. Praise is a kind of spiritual vitamin, a precious 'plus' in life. Lord Chesterfield said, 'I never knew any man deserve praise who did not desire it.'

It is permissible in a social speech to include details of how the organisation started and its principles. But get your facts right first. Make one mistake and you'll find that every member of your audience was listening!

The end

The end is an important part of your speech. It completes it. Don't end with a jerk. If this were other than a social speech, you would summarise, tie up any loose ends, and try to get some action following what you had said. With a social speech, however, you merely repeat your thanks, wish the organisation and its members good luck and, perhaps with a great brotherhood, remind the brethren of the principles that bind them together.

It's often effective to finish with a story.

The specimen speeches in this book, suitably adapted, will cover any social occasion. If the organisation is one about which you know little, have a talk with its secretary or another knowledgeable member. They will supply you with all the information you need, so that, on the day, you will sound erudite. Members take it as a compliment if you show you have some knowledge of their affairs. And in a social speech one of your hopes is that you please your listeners and obtain their applause.

3
Delivering Your Speech

You may have heard the advice: stand up so your audience can see you; speak up so your audience can hear you; then sit down so your audience can enjoy themselves.

Imagine the scene: you stand up and immediately your heart pounds, your legs go rubbery and a mist comes before your eyes. You begin, 'Mr Chairman, ladies and gentlemen...' and are at once breathless. You feel suffocated and miserable, but flounder on, missing much of what you intended saying, until at last it is over. You sit down exhausted, and *you*, far more than your audience, enjoy the fact that you have finished. To your surprise there are cheers, but the cheers seem far off.

You vow: never again! But the gods will no doubt decree otherwise. You'll soon be undergoing the same torture, with the prospect of more doses to come. But it gets better. It really does. There are ways of improving the situation. Soon, far from being terror-stricken when you make a speech, you'll enjoy the experience.

The secret is to *prepare*. Every good public speaker prepares. Those seemingly spontaneous speeches you admire have usually taken hours or days of preparation. Sir Winston Churchill, one of the greatest public speakers of all time, whose speeches galvanised Britain in the hour of need, prepared assiduously. The novice must do her homework if she wishes to succeed.

With a little adaptation of the specimen speeches given later, almost every occasion can be covered. This is true even when making further speeches to the same audience on similar occasions.

To benefit from this book you should select your speech, then make your adaptations to improve it. Next, take it into an unoccupied room.

Stand in the room, feet about 14–18 inches apart, with one foot slightly in front of the other. Try to balance your weight equally on both of them, with a little bias towards the back foot. This is the stance you should try to adopt when speaking, but, whatever you do, don't look stiff and starchy.

Hold your speech in front of you and read aloud. The sound of your voice, this first time, may disconcert or embarrass you. Worse, you may find the style and sentences of a speech written by someone else difficult. If so, rewrite it, using your own phraseology. This will help, because now there is something of yourself in it. Indeed, it is always wiser to alter the samples to your own words, for in that way you are identified with them.

Try to keep your sentences short. Before an audience you may find at first that you become breathless. Short sentences are then easier and your audience will find them simpler to follow. Make your speech a second time in the empty room. It should be easier.

If you are satisfied with the result, read it again, giving your voice the same volume as you would when you are to deliver it.

Speak slowly. This is important. New speakers rush too quickly. They tend to gabble and the effect is consequently lost. Go carefully, pausing for breath as required.

It's not recommended at this stage that you should test yourself with a tape recorder. Only very good ones faithfully reproduce your voice. Many of the small cassette machines to be found in homes – even in these technological times – will not have the degree of fidelity to give you a true reproduction of the way you sound, and may therefore distort your self-appraisal.

Also, even with a good recorder, you will find, on hearing your recorded voice for the first time, that it sounds different – horribly different. This is because in normal speech you hear your voice through the vibrations in your head. This gives it a different 'complexion' altogether. Console yourself with the thought that what you are hearing from the tape recorder is the same voice your friends have been hearing issuing from your lips all your life.

If you must hear your voice and don't have a good machine, cup your hands around your ears and speak aloud. That is pretty much what your voice sounds like.

After several practice runs, set about familiarising yourself with your speech. Some learn their speeches by heart and recite them on the night; others find this too much trouble and prefer to deliver either from the manuscript or from notes of its salient points. In the end, it will be what works for *you*, and it will take some trial and error to arrive at the optimum arrangement.

Double-space your manuscript and be generous with paragraphing. When you read the specimens in this book, you may think there are too many paragraphs. But these are speeches, not mere pieces of writing. They've been set down so that, on the night, your eyes can alight with ease on any line that evades the memory.

Try underlining paragraphs that might have given you trouble in rehearsal, so that, if they *are* elusive on the night, your eye will find them and you'll be able to refresh your memory without searching for the place.

You may find it useful to run over your speech in your mind before dropping off to sleep a few nights before the date. This should help it to sink into the subconscious mind. In the morning, try running over it mentally again. It's surprising the effect this technique has, making learning easier.

If you can't do it with the whole speech, do please try it with your stories. A well-told story will often turn a mediocre speech into a moderate success; your audience almost forgetting its black spots.

Between your first reading of your speech and its delivery on the night, you should read it aloud several times. If you can persuade anyone to listen to it, that helps. Rehearse the speech properly before them in the way you intend to deliver it – standing up and employing whatever gestures or voice modulation you intend to use on the occasion.

With experience, you will discover that you can create effects with your voice by regulating the speed at which you speak, and varying the time.

Such techniques are practised by actors. Although it could be argued that an after-dinner speaker is rather a cross between a lecturer and a music-hall comedian, it's beyond the scope of this book to discuss this in detail. To learn more, listen to speakers on television and you'll discover how professionals get their effects. You'll also find books specifically aimed at voice improvement.

On the night, look your smartest, and don't wear a row of pens in your breast pocket, or anything that might distract attention from what you are saying.

When called upon to speak, stand up and push back your chair so that it doesn't press against you or interfere with the ease of your stance.

Place your feet 14–18 inches apart for good balance as you did when you were rehearsing. Hold your speech in front of you, your thumbs in the margins. Take a deep breath, smile at your audience and start, 'Mr Chairman, ladies and gentlemen...' It could be, '*Madam* Chairman' or, depending on the degree of formality and tradition demanded by the organisation, even 'Madam Chair'. Although this sounds a little strange, even in these politically correct times, it is an opening often used by speakers who wish to avoid sexism.

But back to the manuscript. As you progress, work your thumbs down the page to indicate the place. Consult your manuscript as often as you please, but do look around your audience, and try to project your voice so that it can be heard at the back of the room.

Should you get applause or laughter, pause until it is over. After a funny story, allow a moment for the normal reaction and pray that it will come.

Try to avoid using your notes when telling a story. If you can't, then consult your notes up to your punchline, but *do ensure that you deliver the punchline looking at your audience*.

Don't be tempted to wander from your manuscript. If

you do, you will probably go astray and make a mess of trying to recover.

If you leave a bit of your speech out, don't worry; your audience may never notice.

Try to maintain the volume of your voice throughout so that your audience can hear every word. Try near the end to finish with something of a flourish. Then sit down at once.

Some speakers look at the table for a few seconds once they've sat down; or, if there's a drink handy, help themselves to a much-needed draught before once again looking at the people.

If you're nervous about starting, remember that so is every good speaker and actor. It's not until they're underway and lost in what they have to say that they forget themselves and their audience.

Part 2
The Speeches

4

Introduction

'My sermon on the meaning of manna in the wilderness can be adapted to almost any occasion, joyful, or, as in the present case, distressing. I have preached it at harvest celebrations, christenings, confirmations, on days of humiliation and festal days. The last time I delivered it was at the cathedral, as a charity sermon on behalf of the Society for the Prevention of Discontent among the Upper Orders. The Bishop, who was present, was much struck by some of the analogies I drew.'

So spoke Canon Chasuble in Oscar Wilde's *The Importance of Being Earnest*.

The speeches that follow contain many epigrams, stories and anecdotes. These, like a cat, can have many lives and can, like Canon Chasuble's sermon on the meaning of manna in the wilderness, be adapted to almost any occasion. There are also suggestions for further or alternative ones tacked on the end. So now is the time to explain how to use the collection that follows.

First, gather all the information you can relating to the occasion upon which you are to speak, and write it down. You might call this your preliminary information. Next, you might consult the indexes of this book and find if there is anything in them relevant to your preliminary information. If so, abstract it and add it to your collection.

Then is the time to mull over all this, using your imagination. Eventually, you should be able to abstract from it what you think will convey what you want to say in an interesting and amusing fashion. From this you can write your speech.

You will, eventually, evolve your own methods, but the above procedure is tried and tested, and you could do far worse than stick to it until your own preferred style of working asserts itself.

5

Wedding Speeches –
The Bride's Father

The next few chapters are devoted to wedding speeches, as these are the likeliest that most people will be asked to deliver. First, those for the bride's father, then the bridegroom and then the best man, for that is generally the order in which they are expected to speak at weddings. The bride's father toasts the bride and groom, the bridegroom replies on behalf of himself and the bride, and toasts the bridesmaids, and the best man responds to the toast to the bridesmaids.

Frequently, a friend of the bride's family speaks instead of its head – and so there are some speeches for him or her, as well as for the bridegroom's father, who occasionally speaks. Alternatively, the following speeches specifically for the bride's father may, with suitable adaptation, be used by a substitute speaker.

Many of the speeches contain epigrams and stories. By transferring these from one speech to another, the average person should have ample material for all the weddings at which he may have to speak. Additional material can be found in the jokes and anecdotes section.

Let us begin, then, with speeches for the first to speak: the bride's father.

Bride's father's speech No 1

It gives me great pleasure to wish Jack and Jill every happiness in their married life.

Today my wife and I formally welcomed Jack into our family as a son. Actually he assumed this role some time ago. Because we knew of Jill's feelings for him we were glad to do so.

Jill and he did not keep any of us too long in suspense once they decided they were really meant for each other.

They haven't been a bit like a couple I was told about when my wife and I were arranging today's wedding ceremonies.

This couple had been courting for thirty years. Every evening during that time the man called on the woman at her comfortable home. She would make him a big supper and afterwards they would sit together before a lovely fire. One evening, however, after supper, as they were sitting down looking into the fire, the woman said, 'John, don't you feel it's about time we started thinking about getting married?'

'Married!' exclaimed John. 'Good heavens, who will have us now?'

The other day I overheard a young man asking some friends whether married men live longer than bachelors. Before anyone else had a chance to reply a gloomy-looking man retorted: 'No, it only seems longer!'

My wife is here, so I hastily add that he was quite wrong. Statistics prove that married men do live longer than bachelors... honestly!

But maybe that gloomy-looking man had, that morning, quarrelled with his wife. That being so, his outlook would be prejudiced.

Arguments between husbands and wives do take place, I'm afraid. And married people occasionally have differences. It's undoubtedly a very good thing to be prepared for such occasions at the beginning of marriage and have an arrangement to avoid quarrelling at such times.

I heard a healthy-looking man say at a wedding some time ago that he and his wife had just such an arrangement. 'When a quarrel's starting,' he said, 'one of us immediately leaves the house.' He paused and added unexpectedly, 'That's why I look so well. I get plenty of fresh air!'

Undoubtedly, this man was attending that wedding without his wife. Not content with giving us the reason for his robust appearance he went on to say that he had been married for twenty years.

'When I married my wife,' he said, 'I thought she was an angel. And I still think so. I've got three reasons for this. Firstly, she's always up in the air. Secondly, she's never got anything to wear. And lastly, she's always harping on about something.'

You can all see my wife is here! I don't call her an angel. I don't want her to fly away. I enjoy married life. I like my home comforts. At home I am a man of peace. After you've learnt about marriage strategy, you'll find that's the safest way!

Jack, Jill, we wish you every happiness. Make up your minds to be happy, the two of you, and you *will* be happy.

Ladies and gentlemen, will you please stand up and drink a toast to the health, wealth and happiness of Jack and Jill?

Bride's father's speech No 2

Everyone knows that very popular wedding hymn 'Love divine, all loves excelling. Joy of Heaven to Earth come down.' And everyone here hopes and prays that this is how this marriage will be. Indeed we are confident it will be woven of pure unbound love, freely given and joyfully received.

But I will not pretend that some people – cynics of course – feel that there ought always to be a *second* wedding hymn. It is, however, seldom sung at weddings, but with the gift of prophecy maybe often should be.

And what *is* that hymn?

'Fight the good fight with all thy might'.

I am very pleased to tell you that the one which will be appropriate for your married life depends little, if at all, on fate – it depends on you.

Yes, Jack and Jill, your marriage will be what you make it, I'm glad to say.

We, your friends and relatives, have come here today to pray that it will be your paradise.

When Jack came to ask me for Jill's hand – oh yes, he very properly did that. He is really quite a splendid chap you know.

Anyhow, from that day I have been going around asking friends if they have any helpful words which I could pass on to them when I came to make my speech today.

Here are a few of those – er – topical tips which, incidentally, have passed the – er – censor – who, as Jack already knows, is my better half.

'The bonds of matrimony are not worth much if the interest is not kept up.'

'Man has his will but woman has her way.'

'Woman will be the last thing civilised by man.'

'Love is nature's second sun.'

'It is impossible to love and be wise.'

'Discreet wives have sometimes neither eyes nor ears.'

'Keep your eyes wide open before marriage and half-shut afterwards.'

And finally, a little prayer should help the two of you:

'Please God, give me the serenity to accept the things I cannot change, the courage to change the things I can, and the wisdom to know the difference.'

Jack and Jill, may your love for one another, so evident for all to see today, continue all the days of your life, and may God bless you with health, wealth and happiness.

Ladies and Gentlemen, I give you the toast of 'The Bride and Bridegroom'.

Bride's father's speech No 3

'Marriages are made in heaven.' So goes an old proverb. We all hope that this is so, and particularly that this one today is registered there.

This morning we witnessed a solemn ceremony in church, which our forefathers have revered and in which they have participated for hundreds of years.

And touchingly beautiful it was – the decorated church, the moving words of the ritual, the marvellous music.

There, reverentially, before their God, Jack and Jill pledged themselves to one another for all time. These were moments of magic, of wonder. They were divine.

That was Part One of this wedding.

What I like to think of as Part Two is taking place here and now. This is the part at which their friends add their seal to the pledges made this morning in church.

And when we part from here the marriage will truly have taken place before God and their fellow men and women. Long may it prosper.

It is during this second part of the ceremony that we, the witnesses of this morning's dedication, get to know one another, get to know better the friends and relatives of our new son and our daughter. Indeed, those who are responsible for this get-together – Jack and Jill – may themselves be meeting some of their new relatives for the first time. May they approve of one another. They will, I feel sure, do their best, remembering that first impressions are tremendously important in friendships. We will all do our best to create the atmosphere for it. We hope that the new friendships made today at this wedding between Jack's family and ours will create understanding and affection between our two families.

We welcome Jack into our family and we are glad to believe that his family are doing the same for our beloved daughter.

No doubt, as we get to know each other, there will be a little adjusting to do on both sides.

The other day I heard about a lord who had allowed the ground of his stately home to be used for a cricket match in connection with the village's carnival week, and even promised to take part in it. He himself was batting and his butler umpiring, when suddenly there was a crack and the ball had hit his lordship's cricket pad.

'Howzat!' shouted the bowler.

Boldly the umpire announced, 'His lordship is not at home.'

His lordship looked aghast.

'What the devil do you mean by that?' he demanded. The umpire eyed him as only butlers can.

'I mean that you are out.'

There are bound to be little adjustments and changes to make in our two families, but with a little good will on both sides I am certain they will be taken in our stride.

My toast, ladies and gentlemen, is that of 'The Bride and Bridegroom'. God bless their marriage.

Jack Sprat could eat no fat;
His wife could eat no lean.
So it came to pass between them both
They lived together all serene.

Which is not exactly how this verse of the old nursery rhyme actually ends, but my new last line makes it the best advice to newlyweds I can give.

An American poet put it rather better with, 'A good husband makes a good wife.'

My wife and I think we have made a good daughter. It's up to you, Jack, to make a good wife of her.

But it's up to the two of you to make it a good marriage. No one but your two selves can do that.

We, who have passed the learner stage, and had some time to look around, had time to consider the most fascinating Human Scene, will tell you that one of the great secrets of a happy marriage is Give and Take.

Yes, *both*.

And remember, it is sometimes harder to learn to take.

Joan Sprat might at first have quite liked lean, and possibly deliberately persuaded herself to go off it.

I've noticed that Jack and Jill have already learned something of this lesson. Jill is no longer as keen on some things as she was. And Jack, I'm told, was not always so much the stay-in bird that he's become during the past few months.

During those months, my wife and I have got to know him pretty well. Obviously we approve of the young man we've got to know.

If we hadn't, I would not in church have handed

him our Jill to care for until death them do part. Indeed, had my wife and I not really liked or approved of him I would not have been allowed to give him Jill this morning. That, Jack, is something you'll come to understand as the years go by. Remember, man has his will, but woman has her way. That is how love and understanding will sort it out and it will not be in the least painful.

But I must stop so that the two of you can start getting on with those things for yourselves. Jill is part of our love, experience and understanding, and now that I think of it, it doesn't seem all that long ago since I was teaching her the very nursery rhyme about Jack and Joan Sprat with which I started.

Jack and Jill, may you be as happy as poets would have their lovers. My wife and I will always pray for this, and will do all in our power to make it so

Ladies and gentlemen, will you please rise to drink the most important toast of the day, 'The Bride and Bridegroom'. God bless them both.

Bride's father's speech No 5

Everybody called upon to make a speech, other than your professional spouters, says it! You may not hear the words, but the moment they stand up the words are those dominating the mind.

And I am saying it now: 'Good heavens! I wish someone else were doing this!'

But as the father of the bride I've no choice. It's a must. I must propose the main toast of the day. That of 'The Bride and Groom'. God bless them both. Etiquette says it's the bride's father's privilege. *Privilege?* That's a misnomer if ever there was one. Huh! You should see my knees – perhaps you can hear them knocking, one against the other, to me as loud as castanets.

I wouldn't do this speech thing for anyone other than our own dear daughter, whom today I gave away to Jack.

Oh, I must add that her mother was very much in on it, too! In on it all, from the very beginning. Before I even saw Jack properly.

You bachelors, after you've joined the married state, will soon learn that in matters concerning the family, the wife knows first and best. Yes, I said knows *best!* You must consult her. Moreover, take her advice in these matters.

If you don't, it all goes wrong somehow.

There, that's the first tip I've given you, Jack.

I won't give you any more just now, but should you at any time wish to listen to the Voice of Experience on matters helpful towards – er – matrimonial bliss, Wednesdays are always convenient. Eight o'clock. The wife's out then.

You are now in The Club – the Matrimonial Club – and I can tell you things about life and living you wouldn't understand until now.

You saw the initiation ceremony this morning. Once a man's gone through that, he's in. No matter what, Jack, from now on you've got hundreds of willing listeners. Membership of the Club guarantees them. The only trouble is that most of them really want you to be the listener and when you are they do so go on! If you find they're too much, my advice to the two of you is get yourselves a dog. That'll do all the listening for you – and won't bark your secrets in the street next day, which too many humans just have to do!

One thing I beg of you both. Please, the two of you, don't think of us – your in-laws – as *out*-laws. Indeed, consider as outlaws only those things that might make either of you unhappy.

Don't forget, Jack, a good wife and health are a man's best wealth.

And the most precious possession that ever comes to a man in this world is a woman's heart.

Jill has been a mother's pride and a father's joy.

And with a quotation from Martin Luther, made in 1569, I'll get off my quaking legs.

'There is,' Martin Luther wrote, 'no more lively, friendly and charming relationship, communion or company than a good marriage.'

May yours, Jack and Jill, be such a one, and that is the wish of us all, who now rise and drink to that.

Ladies and gentlemen, I give you the toast of the day, 'Jack and Jill'.

Bride's father's speech No 6

After the solemnity of the marriage service and because we are all a little sad at losing Jack and Jill for a few days, I thought it might be a good idea to try to brighten things up with a few light-hearted remarks.

I'm sure that it's because the wedding ceremony – the giving and taking of one another – is so charged with emotion that wedding receptions with follow-ups like this were invented. They're a sort of balance to what's gone on before. And I can tell you that a great deal of preparation went into this wedding, which, because I myself wasn't as involved as some, I can proudly say was an Oscar-winning performance.

As for me, my main role is to come. Actually it is the most unpleasant connected with the day – I have to pay!

Jill and her mother have, for weeks, been very much afraid that something might go wrong – because actually so much *could* – so they very wisely made a note of these on cards as they occurred to them.

By this morning all these cards except one had been dealt with. This last one Jill gave to me to keep until our car reached the church. Then she asked me for it.

As I handed it to her I noticed that there were three words on it.

These three words named in sequence the places she had to be at for the service. They were *aisle, altar* and *him*.

All of you know the drill. Down the aisle to the altar to stand by him, the bridegroom.

Well, the moment we got inside this church she started saying them like a Hindu mantra.

'Aisle, altar, him; aisle altar him; aisle altar him... I'LL ALTER HIM!'

Marriage is, as everybody knows, a lottery, but if you lose you can't just tear up the ticket and forget about it. Some say the prizes are all blanks. But today Jack has won himself a prize and Jill has by no means drawn a blank. She has got her man – and man, according to a French moralist, is the reason why women don't love one another!

The two of them have from today increased the number of their relatives. For instance, each now has a mother-in-law. And the two brand-new ones here today are splendid ladies, truly well-meaning, no matter what the comics say – and they do say some dreadfully unkind things! Actually, though, one amused me the other day when he said that the heaviest penalty in law for bigamy was getting two mothers-in-law.

But from what I know of Jack and Jill, bigamy is the last thing they're likely to think about. They're so full of one another. Everyone can see that they are terribly in love and idyllically happy.

This fact suddenly struck a young bride as their taxi reached their honeymoon hotel:

'Jack', she said, 'can we pretend to be an old married couple?'

'How?' he said, actually wanting all the world to know... and be warned off.

There was one of those unhelpful pauses, which went on so long that the taxi-driver chipped in.

'You want to look an old married couple? OK, lady, I'll tell you. You carry the cases into the hotel!'

I don't imagine that Jack and Jill will be taking such precautions, but perhaps there are one or two that they should take.

Two newlyweds I heard about last week most certainly wished they had. They were very modern and...er...shall we say, in their own way, rather grand.

They had even fixed themselves up with a new home at which, when they got back from their honeymoon, they gave a housewarming party.

One of the things they boasted about was that they had gone in for *twin* beds. And they made too much of a thing of talking about it, which almost everyone accepted with tongue in cheek.

But the evening was a great success and afterwards letters and phone calls came from everyone.

A week later the two were due to go back to work and so, the following morning, would have to get up early. For this they needed an alarm clock. But where was it?

Eventually, after much searching, the bride had an idea. Her brother had given it to them as a house-warming present. Would *he* remember where she'd put it?

After a while they managed to get him on the telephone. They beat about the bush a bit and came to the point when he was asking his sister whether her husband snored – that sort of thing – with an added, 'How are you doing with the twin beds?'

'Splendidly. They're great,' she said. 'We both sleep like tops.'

Then she added her sixty-four-thousand-dollar question: 'But we need to get up early tomorrow, and can't find the alarm clock you gave us.'

She couldn't understand why he laughed so uncontrollably until he got out, 'I put it in one of your twin beds.'

I'll finish with a quotation from old Will Shakespeare, who always puts things much better than we.

'God, the best maker of marriages, combine your hearts in one.'

Ladies and gentlemen, I give you the toast of the day: 'The Bride and Groom'. God bless them both. If it were not for weddings, many people would never be asked to make a speech.

6
Wedding Speeches –
The Bridegroom

The bridegroom is generally the second to speak. He should include in his speech thanks to the bride's parents and thanks to the guests for their presents, and conclude with a toast to the bridesmaids.

A short speech might go something like the first of those that follow.

Bridegroom's speech No 1

First of all I want to say thank you to all of you for coming to our wedding and joining us here afterwards. My wife and I are delighted to have you here enjoying yourselves with us on this, the happiest day of our lives.

I want to say thank you, too, to everyone who wished us good luck, health and happiness, particularly those who, in doing so, have undergone the ordeal of making a speech.

This seems to me to be an appropriate moment to thank my father and mother for being such splendid parents to me. I only hope that Jill and I make as good a job of our married life as they have of theirs. And...er...that all our children are as nice as I am!

Jill and I are very grateful to those kind people who have given us such excellent presents. Every time we look at them they bring joy to our hearts.

To our splendid best man, our greatest thanks. He has been a great help in helping to organise everything.

Our special gratitude, too, to our delightful bridesmaids, who have contributed so much to the beauty and excellence of this wonderful day.

It is their toast that I now have the privilege and delight to propose. Ladies and gentlemen, 'Our Bridesmaids'.

Bridegroom's speech No 2

Today you witnessed a metamorphosis. It happened to Jill. From a Miss she metamorphosed to a Missus. But Jill is not, as in the musical *Cats,* a cat; to call her a kitten is permissible, but a cat, no!

She's everything that is good, beautiful and wonderful and she's now my beloved wife – and now, seemingly, also starting to look embarrassed...!

Er...ladies and gentlemen, my wife – there, that was the first time for me really to call her that! Ahem... my *wife* and I want to thank all of you for coming to share with us this, our happiest day. And, particularly, I want to thank my new parents. Without them there would be no Jill and without Jill obviously none of us would be here enjoying this super occasion. Today, they have given Jill to me to love and cherish, and to that I will, henceforth, devote my life. We both thank them very much too for this delightful reception, which we are all enjoying immensely. There are other parents we both want to thank, too – mine. They've been wonderful parents to me, and, today, I have partly repaid them by bringing them a new daughter who will, I assure them, be far less troublesome than I have been.

And who knows how long it'll be before I'll be bringing Jill and a newer-still member of the family to add to their happiness? As Tiny Tim said, 'God bless us all!'

Thank you, all of you, too, for giving us such wonderful wedding presents. We do prize them and we are most grateful to you. Bless you.

Jill and I also want to thank my...er...father-in-law. That's *another* new name I've collected today – Jill and I want to thank my father-in-law for the very nice way he's proposed our toast. Thank you...Dad!

And, lastly, we want to say a very, very big thank you to those marvellous young ladies who, next to my bride, are really the most beautiful in the room: our bridesmaids. They've been perfect and a tremendous help. And it is now my great pleasure to propose their very good health and happiness.

Ladies and gentlemen, I give the toast to: 'The Bridesmaids'.

Bridegroom's speech No 3

When I first met Jill...! That was at a disco, and I remember thinking, 'She's nice, very nice...!' But I certainly didn't think that I'd be here today thanking her father for proposing our health as the bride and bridegroom. Our love was not a sudden explosion. It is something that's grown with our tender care and of which neither of us is therefore likely to repent at leisure. We thank you very much, father-in-law, for the kind things you have said, and for so generously being the Founder of this Feast. Many thanks also to my father for doing so much for me.

To our two mothers, too, thanks be for everything. We hope someday to prove that your bid for immortality hasn't been in vain, by perpetuating your genes into generations to come, or – as the King James version of the Bible so quaintly puts it – by multiplying.

And we want to thank those who made our union meet and right: the vicar and all the staff of his beautiful church, which so many of you attended.

Thank you, one and all, for coming here. We hope that you are enjoying yourselves and will continue to do so throughout the day.

You have given us wonderful wedding presents, which we much appreciate. Thank you so much.

Particularly, Jill wants me to thank the bridesmaids, who, she says, have been so kind and helpful to her. Not only today, but throughout the nervous weeks that went in preparation for today. I should like to add mine, too, and say that they look just wonderful.

Already I've noticed naughty twinkles in the eyes of some of the – er – chaps here present. Watch 'em girls. I'm pretty sure that the intentions of some of them are strictly dishonorable. Nevertheless, bear in mind that, play your cards right, and another enchanting day like this can be arranged very easily – to our mutual joy and happiness. So go to it all you eligibles. Wouldn't it be great if all the unmarried here today were, within twelve months, like us, married...and blissfully happy?

Ladies and gentlemen, I give you the toast of these marvellous young ladies who are our bridesmaids.

'The Bridesmaids'.

Bridegroom's speech No 4

If, as the worldly-wise say, marriage is a lottery, then I am a winner, and have got the first prize, which has made me the happiest of men.

I am the luckiest, too, to have won Jill, who will now have to get used to being called Mrs Smith. Sounds good, doesn't it? It gets all my bells ringing, anyway!

And that's not the total of my good luck.

There are Jill's parents, who are our generous hosts here today. Mine, too, who have been such good parents to me. I'm very lucky to have them. I couldn't have chosen better myself!

Then there are you – yes, all of you. You are not just a lucky dip among my acquaintances, but a treasure chest of those friends whom Jill and I regard as the priceless jewels of our lives.

Thank you, all of you, for coming, and for the splendid presents which you have given us.

And lastly – one keeps one's best thanks, like one's goodies, until the end. Lastly, there are our adorable bridesmaids. Today they are the most scintillating jewels in our treasure chest. They look lovely don't they? But, believe me, they're not mere decorations to this occasion. Jill says she doesn't know what she would have done without them - their help, advice and support. Not only today, but during the preparations in the weeks that have gone by.

It is now my great pleasure to propose their toast. Ladies and gentlemen, I ask you to be upstanding and drink heartily the toast of: 'The Bridesmaids'.

Bridegroom's speech No 5

My wife and I... There, I've said it! You knew I would, didn't you? Well, I couldn't resist saying it and I knew you'd all be disappointed if I didn't. So I just had to say it. Though I must admit, it does sound odd when you say it out loud for the first time.

Anyway, my wife and I – that is, of course, *Jill* and I – want to thank you for coming to our wedding and for all the lovely presents you've given us.

Particularly, we want to thank Jill's parents for this

splendid reception. You know, I can't understand why they're so nice and kind to me, for in reality I am the thief who came and stole their daughter.

I do, however, promise them to do my best to be worthy of her, and to make her as happy as I can.

My parents? Well, I can never thank them properly for being so good to me.

It seems that today I've become a much more worthy person. I now have a better half, a help-mate, a consort, a spouse; and I myself am a Lord and Master! Phew!

Lord and Master? Well, there's no harm in kidding oneself, is there?

Even so, permit me to remind you of what one of the great sex symbols of our time, the actress Marilyn Monroe, had to say on this.

She said, 'I don't mind living in a man's world as long as I can be a woman in it.'

The film star Marilyn Monroe was herself a beauty, and there's a lot of that here today in addition to my bride, who alone surpasses our delightful bridesmaids, whose toast I am about to propose.

We are very grateful to them for all the help they've given us so freely, and for being so charming to everyone, particularly our parents. Thank you very much, all of you. You've made this a wonderful day.

And now, may I ask you please to raise your glasses and drink heartily the toast to the bridesmaids.

'The Bridesmaids!'

Bridegroom's speech No 6

This is the loveliest, the happiest, the most joyous day of my life.

Thank you all for helping to make it so – by coming! Lord Byron, who knew a thing or two about love, joy and happiness, put it rather well with this:

All who joy would wish
Must share it – Happiness was born a twin
So pass this on. Make my happiest day yours too.

Everyone has been most kind to Jill and me, and we thank you, all of you, but especially our parents for producing us, for rearing us, and for bringing us up to this, our happiest day.

To all of you who're here and have given us such lovely presents, thank you. We'll have such happy times when we return from our honeymoon talking about them, and about this day, to you, their donors.

During our honeymoon we'll send all of you cards...we hope! If you don't receive them, don't be disappointed...and don't really blame the Post Office. It's the thought that counts. And you know about people in love, how it takes them away from reality, blissfully into wonderland, which is where Jill and I will be. It's a place where people can't find time to write, no matter how they wish to tell their friends and relations how enchanting it all is. Think of us, please, as lovers in love, and forgive our neglect.

We want to say thank you especially to our bridesmaids and my best man. Without them we would have been lost. They've certainly smoothed our path. Actually this toast is only to the bridesmaids.

What did Tennyson say about bridesmaids? Wasn't it, 'A happy bridesmaid makes a happy bride?' And Jill is happy, very happy – look at her!

I can't find anything that the poets have said about the best man. And, between ourselves, although mine

51

has performed his duties in the most exemplary manner, he is the only one here complaining.

'Why,' he asks, 'do the bridesmaids get a toast, but not me, the best man?'

He's got a point there, we must admit. And, as I said, he's carried out his duties and looked after me in an exemplary fashion – a really splendid fellow.

Between ourselves – *better* than I expected. I anticipated at least one practical joke from him. Such as at the altar, when the organ was booming forth the wedding march and the bride's party was advancing upon us, a whisper in my ear: 'Jack, I can't find the ring. Have you got it?' Imagine how I'd have felt! Panic, did someone say? God help me!

I'm very lucky in that Jill likes him, too, which means that he, like the bridesmaids, will always be welcome at our home, which some sage has said is the wife's castle.

Actually, as I have said, this is the toast to the bridesmaids, but I would, if I may, like to couple it with one to our best man.

Ladies and gentlemen, will you please stand, raise your glasses and drink to: 'The Bridesmaids and the Best Man!'

7

Wedding Speeches –
The Best Man

The best man is usually the third to speak, and responds to the toast just proposed by the groom (that of the bridesmaids). It is often assumed that the best man's speech has to be a laugh-a-minute affair, but forced humour can often backfire and leave the speaker with a red face staring at a lot of *blank* ones – and a room full of embarrassing silence.

Tell jokes only if you are good at it. No one *expects* you to have them rolling in the aisles. A well-balanced story intended to produce smiles or a gentle titter will more easily find its mark in most cases. If you *are* a stand-up comic by profession, then jokes – and 'the way I tell 'em' – will be more important.

Best Man's speech No 1

I wonder if anybody at this wedding knows why I'm called the Best Man. Surely the best man here today is the bridegroom? It's his day, not mine. I'm here to look after him until he goes on his honeymoon. And after that I have the delightful duty of looking after the bridesmaids.

Things weren't always so. Generations ago, the best man had to marry the bride if the groom failed to attend the wedding. In those days his title was, in my opinion, more appropriate: he was then called the *second*-best man.

I haven't discovered why this custom fell into

disuse. Maybe too many bachelors refused to become second-best men. Or perhaps brides-to-be found those who risked it were almost always unsuitable, and caused a scene.

I suppose, though, that the first of these reasons is the true one, for isn't a bachelor a man who tries to avoid the issue?

But I'm not a confirmed bachelor. I don't think the only marriage that can be justified is the one that produced me. I approve of this one today, and wish Jack and Jill every bit of good luck.

I approve of their marriage for another reason, too. Haven't they made me their best man? And haven't I, in consequence, the pleasure of looking after these charming bridesmaids?

Our bride looks beautiful, and Jack already looks the dutiful husband. The two will always remember this day, and, from time to time, will think about all of us who are here, making it the wonder that it is.

In responding to the toast to your lovely bridesmaids, I wish you, Jack and Jill, the best in health, wealth and happiness – and, when you come to consider your next big investment together, may we hopefully point out that there's nothing like putting your money into...livestock!

Ladies and gentlemen, I think I have gone on long enough. On behalf of the bridesmaids, I say thank you very much.

Best Man's speech No 2

I'm enjoying this wedding. Everything's gone as smoothly as clockwork. The threatened rain's kept away. Instead, the sun's shone throughout the proceedings.

And on such beauty! Everyone's either in their Sunday best or a very special wedding outfit –

enchanting, radiant! Say what you will, but fine feathers do make fine birds, don't they?

The bride and bridesmaids are the prettiest of pictures. Indeed, many pictures have been taken of them – and, like you, I've made sure of getting copies. It's the loveliest of days.

Everyone's happy. Even those of us who have speeches to make!

The bridegroom looks super, too, doesn't he? Until I handed him the ring in church he was my responsibility, you know. Now Jill has him, and I have prettier charges than him – our bridesmaids. Admire them – there's no extra charge.

Beautiful, aren't they? They are my responsibility and I am their chief escort. Best man's perks, you know! I'm delighted with them.

We're enjoying ourselves so much – they and I – that we beg you, Jack and Jill, to invite us to all your other weddings. We've decided that you must have two at least – perhaps three. You both seem strong and fit enough for the course. I'm not advocating bigamy, but am referring to anniversaries – silver, ruby and golden weddings, of course. At those, we hope that little strangers will have multiplied into second and third generations; more, if Jack and Jill get on with it and don't waste time.

And, if you're ever in need of babysitters, try us – your bridesmaids and best man. We're hopeful and willing.

And now it's my most pleasant duty to reply to the toast to the bridesmaids and best man, charmingly proposed by Jack and so enthusiastically received by you. Our bridesmaids have greatly enjoyed being there and meeting all of you. They are grateful to each and all of you for making them so welcome, and the day itself a perfect day.

Thank you all very much.

When Jack asked me to be his best man and I said 'Yes', I didn't know that the best man had to make a speech. Well I'm a bachelor and have kept away from weddings. Nobody told me about the speechmaking until last week. It was too late then for me to do anything about it.

A week before the invitations went out, I might have managed to persuade Jack to get Jill to elope. That way no one would have to undergo the tortures of making or listening to speeches.

But then we wouldn't be having this do, either. Moreover, Jack and Jill wouldn't be getting wedding presents – those gifts that, in the years to come, will remind them of this wonderful day and of their many friends.

Can't win, can we?

I think Jack is, in all fairness, bound to say that, unaccustomed as I am to these things, I've coped with all the best man's duties pretty well. Well, nothing's actually gone wrong, that is, not yet, anyway, and I'm keeping my fingers crossed – and so's Jack.

So maybe you'll let me off this speechifying hook lightly and not expect too many words from me.

You nice people don't really want to hear me at all, I'm sure. It's this bogey called convention that's the trouble. This doing things proper!

We all came to witness the joining together of Jack and Jill, the making of two into one, and touchingly beautiful it was. We also all came to wish this worthy union everything that is fine, good, desirable and happy.

And no one wishes this more fervently than the bridesmaids and myself. Jack said some very nice things about them as he asked you to drink to their health and happiness, and it is now my pleasant duty on their behalf to reply to him.

The bridesmaids are very glad to be here today. They much appreciate the kind things you've said about their work and their looks. They've told me that it's good to know that they've given everybody so much pleasure and that they've really enjoyed helping such a stunning bride as Jill.

Their wish and mine is that the bride and groom may have a long and happy life, and, too, that all of you here today may remember them and this happy day for many years.

Thank you one and all.

Best Man's speech No 4
(For someone who is nervous and wants to get his speech finished as soon as he may decently do so, this can be effective.)

Making speeches, as most of you nice people here know, is not my favourite role. On the contrary, the very thought of making one terrifies me – gives me nerves and stomach troubles and upsets me all over. Whenever people try to inflict such a role upon me I reply at once with a point-blank, *No!* Too often I even forget to say thank you for the honour they do in asking me. For it *is* an honour, and, on a day such as this, it's one of the greatest a very special friend can bestow on one.

And I am certainly aware of this and am tremendously grateful for being asked. I will make a strange confession, too: although anticipating making this little speech has for weeks taken a great deal out of me, I wouldn't have liked it if someone else had been asked instead of me. That's life, isn't it?

And so, ladies and gentlemen, the honour of

replying to the bridesmaids toast is mine.

On their behalf I must say thank you very much to the bridegroom for the kind – but, mark you, *deserved* – compliments he's paid them, and to all of you who've gone out of your way to be sweet and kind to them. They're very happy to be here as Jill's bridesmaids, and want me to thank all of you.

Ladies and gentlemen, on behalf of my lovely charges, thank you very much.

Best Man's speech No 5

Until Jack and Jill did me the great honour of asking me to be their best man I couldn't understand this best-man business at all.

Surely, I said to myself, the *bridegroom* is the best man – the bravest, the luckiest, most desired man.

Not his side-kick, the guy whose only job is to produce the wedding ring at the appropriate time so the groom can pop it on his bride's third finger – left hand.

How wrong one can be! This is the voice of experience.

Just listen to me and maybe you'll have second thoughts about who's the best man...

First of all, the best man must be a bachelor.

They daren't ask a married man. Married men are experienced, know what it's all about.

Bachelors know nothing of those mysteries that convert a miss into a missus, or of the endless preparations that go into managing this.

For the information of those who haven't had the experience, let me tell you.

A best man is some kind of Boy Scout. You know, a chap brimming over with bonhomie, dedicated to good turns – that sort of man.

This paragon – yes, that's what I am! – this paragon must be brave, have the kind of bravery that falters not when sorting out all kinds of intimidating people, from harassed vergers to irate traffic wardens and including demanding dowagers or their ogre husbands.

He must make the path seem straight and even when really it's not a path at all, but a burning deck with a cargo of snakes.

He is the bridegroom's steadying influence, the cheerful chap who sees to everything, and keeps his head in all the emergencies.

Responsibilities – dear me, I'll tell you. Do you know, I didn't dare let myself go even at last night's stag? There was so much to do this morning.

The best man is responsible for getting the groom to church on time. Yes, the best man has to help dress the groom; see to it that his pockets don't bulge with the usual paraphernalia.

And then I had to make sure that we had extra handkerchiefs – a vicar told me to see to *that* one!

Above all, I had to make sure of the ring. All Jack did was keep asking about it. I nearly had a nervous breakdown checking again and again that it was actually in my pocket.

Had I taken it out, even once, I'm sure I'd have lost it.

You've no idea of what I went through before we got to the church – the strain of it.

But all that disappeared miraculously in church. My worries melted away the moment our enchanting bride arrived with her wonderful retinue.

Beauty and light came in with the bride and her lovely bridesmaids.

Since their arrival, all has been well, very well with me.

Feast your eyes upon them, ladies and gentlemen. They are charm itself. As soon as they appeared, the scene changed, everything became sweetness and light, and I became the happiest of mortals. They are my good fairies. In their presence the snakes dare not materialise.

And so, ladies and gentlemen, it is, on their behalf, my great pleasure to thank Jack for the super way in which he proposed the toast of the bridesmaids, who, like myself, wish Jill and you everything that is best in the new life that you're now starting.

Best Man's speech No 6 (A brief one)

Actually, when Jack asked me to make this speech I had the grace not even to pretend to say no. Instead, I said, 'What must I say?'

He gave me one of his despairing looks then said, 'I've got to propose the toast to the bridesmaids and you have to reply to it.'

I must have looked bewildered for he went on, 'That means just say thank you'.

And I am very glad to do that, ladies and gentlemen. Our charming bridesmaids are very grateful to you for the courteous way with which all of you have treated them and for the many compliments you've paid them. Compliments for their beauty, taste, dress, decorum, indeed everything. They love you too. On behalf of these delightful, beautiful young ladies who have done so much to make this a red-letter day which will be remembered always by everyone here, thank you one and all very much.

8

Other Wedding Speeches

Speeches by the bride's father, the bridegroom and best man are all that are usually required at weddings nowadays, but sometimes the bride's father is absent and/or prefers someone else to deputise, or else a fourth speech may be expected from someone representing the bridegroom's family. One of the following may be suitable.

Extra wedding speech no 1

William Penn, years after he'd added Pennsylvania to our empire, wrote:

> *Never marry but for love;*
> *But see that thou lovest what is lovely.*

Both Jack and Jill have done that as we all can see, and today they're at their best.

They have not married in haste, but have gone through, shall we say, the proper channels. They will not, therefore, according to the sages, repent at leisure.

In the 17th century the makers of proverbs were saying, 'Marry first and love will follow.'

Jack and Jill, there can be nothing but bliss in store for you, provided that you bear in mind another ancient proverb, which tells us that,

> *Marriage with peace is this world's paradise;*
> *With strife, this life's purgatory.*

Remember what the poet William Cowper said, 'A disputable point is no man's land', and you'll always have peace. Emerson gave another piece of helpful advice: 'Let a man behave in his own house as a guest.'

About the same time, another American observer of the human scene was very perceptively writing, 'Man has his will but woman has her way.'

A wife should always remember that a man is happy to be king or peasant, who finds peace in his home.

Jack and Jill, now that you are both prisoners of wedlock, and about to set up your own home, I hope you'll find what others have said about that helpful.

Let's start with Cervantes: 'You are a king by your own fireside, as much as any monarch on his throne.'

Kipling in his *Our Lady of the Snows* gives us the experience of one lady:

'Daughter am I in my mother's house, but mistress in my own.'

A more contemporary author has observed perceptively that 'A man's home is his wife's castle.'

And finally there is Emerson again:

'The ornament of a house is the friends who frequent it.'

To the two of you, Jack and Jill, I would wish the serenity to accept the things you cannot change, the courage to change the things you can, and the wisdom to know the difference.

May God bless the two of you and give you health, wealth and happiness all the days of your life.

Extra wedding speech No 2 (Honeymoon)

In a little while Jack and Jill will be leaving us to go

on their honeymoon, which I am told is also sometimes called 'honey *month*'. Traditionally it lasted a whole month and was commonly spent in travelling before settling down to the business of life.

May their honeymoon be the best, most enjoyable holiday of their lives.

Here, maybe, I should, however, strike a cautionary note and tell them about the newlyweds who went to the seaside for their honeymoon.

On being shown the door of their room in the hotel, the young husband gallantly picked up his bride and carried her across the threshold. A week later, when they were leaving, she supported him to the lift and carried him out to their waiting taxi.

But love seems to've addled the minds of that couple, for when they first entered their hotel bedroom she uttered a little cry of dismay as she saw that there were twin beds.

'What's the matter, darling?' he asked anxiously.

Already there was a tear in her eyes and she answered, with a catch in her voice, 'Darling, you told me we were going to have a room to ourselves!'

The following morning he took her to the beach and as they watched the waves he began to quote Byron:

'Roll on, thou dark and deep blue ocean, roll!'

'Darling,' she interrupted him. 'Oh, you are wonderful. Look, it's doing it!'

The season wasn't yet properly started and their small hotel was having some difficulty in recruiting staff, so the service wasn't all that it could be.

On their first evening they decided to have their baths before dinner. He went to the bathroom at the end of the corridor and she to the one almost next door to their bedroom, saying that it would take her much longer than him, and that she would see him later for a pre-dinner drink in the cocktail bar.

He'd had several drinks when she arrived, almost two hours later.

He looked at his watch. 'Darling,' he expostulated, 'surely you don't take two hours for a bath.'

Tears welled up in her eyes. 'There was no curtain in the bathroom,' she sobbed, 'and I had to keep getting out to breathe on the window.'

Before the end of the week her mother sent them their local paper in which there was an account of their wedding. Mother-in-law had underlined the last few words of that, and added a note which read, 'I'm sure he deserved it.'

The last few words of the paper's wedding report were, 'The gift of the bride to the bridegroom was a beautiful dressing-down.'

I began with a word of caution and now, so as to balance these few words, my last words are of caution too.

'Always remember that the critical period in matrimony is breakfast time, and also that any mud thrown is ground lost.'

I know that you're much more with it than the couple I've been telling you about. Their experiences will not be yours, but it's never a bad thing to say to oneself, 'There, but for the grace of God, go I.'

And may God go with you, not only on your honeymoon but all the days of your life.

Bless you both.

Because at weddings it is the men who usually make the speeches most of these have been written from a man's point of view and frequently poke good-natured fun at the ladies. The one that follows is different. It is one that's very much for the ladies. It should be delivered in friendly tones and in a not-too-serious manner, preferably by

64

someone devoted to women's rights.

If one of the male guests makes it he could exonerate himself by beginning with, 'Jill's mother feels that nowadays there's always too much pandering to the bridegroom's sex – *our* sex! – at weddings, and insisted that someone should favour the ladies with kind supportive words. Because I am already a member of the family I have been elected to do so.' (Or, 'Because I am married I have, by my wife, here present, been elected to do so!')

Extra wedding speech No 3

Ladies and gentlemen,

Today, Jack, in getting Jill to marry you, you've done inordinately well for yourself.

Let me quote for you what that renowned Victorian novelist Charles Reade had to say about a wife:

'A wife is essential to great longevity: She is the receptacle of half a man's cares and two-thirds of his ill-humour.'

An Irish bishop named Jeremy Taylor, centuries earlier, wrote, 'A married man falling into misfortune is more apt to retrieve his situation in the world than a single one, chiefly because his spirits are soothed and retrieved by domestic endearments, and his self-respect kept alive by finding that, although all abroad be darkness and humiliation, yet there is a little world of love over which he is monarch.'

Ladies and gentlemen, take notice particularly. Those are not the words of two women's libbers. Indeed, their authors had been mouldering in their graves decades before those greatest of women, the sufragettes, were making their heroic stand.

Go farther back still to the days when the Chinese were making proverbs for the world.

'A hundred men', says one of those, 'may make an

encampment, but it takes a woman to make a home.'

Now, what would you say was the sex of the person who said that, 'If a woman can be a sweetheart, valet, audience, cook and nurse, she is qualified for marriage'? Don't bother to answer. It's obvious. But isn't it also true?

As we were standing outside the church this morning, watching Jack and Jill being photographed, a passer-by stopped to look, and asked me, 'Do you think she'll make him a good wife?'

'She will,' I said. And I can bet you, all of you, here present, what else she'll make him too. She'll *make him a good husband!*

Far too frequently imputations are made regarding the fair sex without even the slightest justification. They hurt, you know.

Remarks like saying the fair sex should be called the *un*fair sex.

Or trotting out dubious definitions such as, 'A bachelor is often a man who's been crossed in love; but a married man is one who's been *double-*crossed.'

Then there is the mischievous practice of relating snide stories such as the one in which the foreman asks the new shop steward, 'Did my wife speak at this morning's staff meeting?'

To which the shop steward replies, 'I don't know your wife, Foreman. But a tall, fair lady did get up and say that she couldn't find words to express her feelings, and...'

There, the foreman cuts him short. 'Couldn't find words to express her feelings, did you say? That certainly wasn't my wife!'

Here's another, a similar humbug.

In this the wife is made to say, 'I think married men should wear something to show they're married.'

That goads her miserable little husband to protest, 'I *do* wear something that shows that I'm married: this shiny suit!'

A more realistic picture of the domestic scene is conjured up by tales similar to the one about the poor wife who's wakened at night by noises downstairs. Scared, she turns to her husband, who's at her side, and whispers, 'I think there are burglars downstairs. Are you awake?'

Stiff with fright, he says, 'No!'

Or there's this typical illustration of the way so many wives are treated.

'John, I can't stand much more of this. You don't consider me at all. I'm sick and tired of your carrying on as though I weren't here. You've been out at work all day and I've been here, on my own, with no one to talk to. And now that you *are* home you just sit there reading your old paper, taking no notice at all of me...! You don't love me any more. That's it, isn't it?'

And her Lord and Master stirs himself to say, 'Darling, that's utter nonsense. Every time you come near me you turn me on. Every day, I love you more and more. Honestly, I worship the ground on which you walk. Your every wish is my command...! But, for Pete's sake, let me get on with reading my horoscope!'

To you who are already married, I offer this piece of advice; take it or leave it, but I urge you to take it.

Try praising your wife – even if, at first, it frightens her.

I started with words written by a one time bishop of Down and Connor, and will end with another quotation from him.

'A good wife is heaven's best gift to men – his gem of many virtues, his casket of jewels. Her voice is sweet music, her smiles his brightest day, her kiss the guardian of his innocence, her arms the pale of his safety, her industry his surest health, her economy his safest steward, her lips his faithful counsellors, her bosom the safest pillow of his cares.'

To you, Jack and Jill, our very best wishes.

Soon, you will be safely off on your honeymoon; may it be all for which you hope, and splendid in every way.

As for me – poor me! Well, after my little speech, is there, *please*, here, some kind Amazon who'll escort me to the sanctuary of her hearth, where I'll be safe from vengeful chauvinists for the rest of the day?

Extra wedding speech No 4 (A sailor's viewpoint)

We've been to church and afterwards listened to worthy speeches, all of which have been excellent – far better than I am capable of delivering. In bed, last night I was considering all this, and got to thinking that, by the time my turn came, Jack and Jill and the rest of us might be a little tired of solemnity, and it might therefore be a good plan to turn aside for a short while from the serious, and tell you something about my Uncle Bill. My Uncle Bill is a sailor – OK, you've never heard of him. That's because we don't talk about him outside the family. The distaff side doesn't approve of him. He's the nearest we've got to a skeleton in the cupboard.

To begin with, I don't think he's actually married, but you know what sailors are.

Of his sailor friends, Uncle Bill sings,

We joined the Navy to see the world
And what did we see?
We saw the sea!

Between ports, according to him, it's all routine and often just sheer boredom. Too much time for thinking, too much time for talking... and too little to think or talk about.

And they only see the distaff side of humanity when they're in port. Deprived. He says he can think of little else. Their talk and thoughts are mostly girls, girls, girls.

As to the question of holy matrimony, everyone knows that in this sailors are gentlemen of considerable experience – for doesn't a sailor have a wife in every port?

Anyway, I thought you might be interested to hear some of the things my naughty Uncle Bill divulged to me.

Oh, Jack and Jill, don't take him too seriously. Remember what sailors are. The saying 'Tell it to the marines' I dare say originated in the fo'castle, as the crew howled down a really tall story. Naïve marines on their first voyage would swallow anything, and like ship's apprentices frequently did – the anchor.

One of the stories he relates is about two sailors who hadn't met for years but now were on the same ship again.

'Jack,' said one to his old friend, who was now the ship's cook, 'tell me, did you marry that blonde in Liverpool you were so mad about, or do you still darn your own socks and do your own washing?'

Jack's face fell. 'Yes,' he said gloomily, 'and I still do.'

The best advice for newly wedded husbands, according to my Uncle Bill, is to act dumb and tell 'em nowt.

Presently Sailor Jack went on to boast about the accomplishments of his blonde wife from Scouse country.

'She can swim, ride, run, drive a car and, next week, is going to learn to glide,' he boasted. 'Really, she's a great all-rounder.'

His friend Tom sniffed and said, 'Then you must get along fine together. With all those things to do, the cooking will obviously be all yours!'

The two friends chatted on and presently Jack asked, 'Any good shows on in port?'

Tom thought a moment, then said, 'There's a hypnotist on at the Alhambra. He hypnotised Jimmy-the-One on Tuesday.'

Jack asked, 'What do you mean, hypnotised?'

'It means getting a man in your power and getting him to do anything you want.'

'That's not hypnotism,' said Jack. 'That's marriage!'

They talked on, reminiscing as old friends do, until presently Jack had the feeling that Tom was giving nothing away while he was telling all.

And so he turned to Tom and said, 'Tell me, how is it that you never got spliced yourself?'

Tom shrugged. 'Well, it's like this. When I was very young I promised my mother – God rest her soul – that I'd never marry until I found the ideal woman. Believe me, I sailed the seven seas before I found her.'

'Oh?' Jack's eyes became saucers. 'And then what?'

'Huh!' Tom's face fell. 'She was looking for the ideal man.'

You have found your ideal man, Jill, and you your ideal woman, Jack. Bless you both.

Take no notice of the silly stories I've told; instead remember:

Grave authors say, witty poets sing,
That honest wedlock is a glorious thing.

I was at a wedding a little while ago and heard a man who'd been married a long time remark, 'Marriage is what you make it.'

I'm sure that this is quite true, but when I tried giving this as a piece of advice to a friend he retorted, 'Yes, it does make two of you one, but it's a lifelong struggle to discover which is the one.'

Even so, the famous Dr Johnson declared, as was his fashion, 'Marriage has many pains, but celibacy has no pleasures.'

A young lady who was sitting next to me at the wedding about which I spoke a moment ago said she'd asked her aunt if, during the many years of her married life, she'd not thought of divorce.

'No,' said her aunt, 'only murder!'

The same young lady went on to say that marriage is popular with men because it combined the maximum of temptation with the maximum of opportunity.

But when she added the crack, 'A good wife laughs at her husband's jokes not because they're clever but because *she* is', I thought it high time I asked a male friend or two what *they* thought. I'm glad to say they were equal to the occasion and retorted with pungency.

Here are a few of their remarks.

'A man's incomplete until he's married, and then he's completely finished.'

'Marriage is like a steaming bath. Once you're in it it's not so hot.'

'Marriage is the difference between painting the town and painting the back porch.'

A very happy looking man remarked, 'I've got the finest wife in the country. I hope she stays there.'

Well, as none of these points of view was really encouraging I decided to extend my enquiries. This time I asked more experienced, more stable people what they thought. This is what they had to say.

'A good marriage is like a good handshake. There's no upper hand.'

'Marriage resembles a pair of shears joined together so they can't be separated. Often they move in opposite directions. But woe betide anyone who comes between them.'

'A good wife is like the ivy that beautifies the building to which it clings, twining its tendrils more lovingly as time converts the ancient edifice into a ruin.'

Personally, I think marriage consists not in two people looking into each other's eyes, but in two people standing shoulder to shoulder, both looking in the same direction, bravely facing whatever life may put in their path.

I'm sure that Jack and Jill will do this.

We all wish them every happiness, health, wealth and good luck.

Ladies and gentlemen, I give the toast of: 'The Bride and Bridegroom'.

Extra wedding speech No 6 (The bridegroom's father)

'By their fruits ye shall know them' is a verse that I often heard quoted at school. Years have passed since those days. During them I've come to realise what a depth of truth that line contains. But it was only the other day that someone quoted for me its corollary. He was telling me about two schoolboy brothers who had broken his window.

'Ah,' he said, 'by their parents ye shall know them!'

It'll be through Jill, what Jill really is, that we shall really get to know Bill and Anne Smith, just as they will really get to know my wife and me through Jack.

We are very glad to be here today. Parents, you know, spend half their time worrying how their children will turn out and the other half wondering when they will turn in. From now on we will know where Jack is turning in!

We thank Bill and Anne for giving him the hand of Jill in marriage and look forward to the day when it bears fruit. Babies not only make two families one; they are also the rivets that keep together the bonds of matrimony.

We welcome Jill into our family. We feel that we're not losing a son but gaining a daughter.

Her parents' happiness is bound to affect Jill, so I ask you to be upstanding and drink to the health and happiness of: 'The Bride's Parents'.

9

Engagement and Stag Parties

Engagement parties, by and large, are far too carefree for formalities. On such occasions people don't want to listen to speeches. They prefer to enjoy themselves in other, more animated ways. If you are called upon to make a speech, the one that follows will be quite sufficient.

The Engagement Party speech

We are, this evening, celebrating the fact that Jack has given Jill an engagement ring. We congratulate the two of them and wish them every joy and happiness.

No one can say that Jill is a gold-digger. In fact, it's Jack who's profiting from their engagement, as by accepting his proposal of marriage Jill's made Jack one of the 'landed' gentry!

Thank you for asking us to join you tonight. We're grateful to you for your friendship, which will, we trust, live on, come what may.

A cynic said to me the other day that an engagement was the time a girl takes to find out if she can do any better.

This is quite untrue of Jill. She's looking forward with eagerness to the day when Jack gives her another ring – a wedding ring. We hope to be around then, to bless them both and wish them good luck.

And we hope to be around shortly after that, when Jack buys yet another ring. Again, we will bless and congratulate them.

That third ring? What will it be? Why, a teething

ring, of course!

I give you the toast to Jack and Jill. May God be good to them and grant them health and happiness. 'To Jack and Jill!'

Stag parties! It's a puzzling name for a celebration. But one dictionary has it as 'Stag-dance-party: A dance or party of men only', and gives 'stigai' as the Icelandic origin of the root, meaning to mount. This is fair enough, but what would the bridegroom's friends say if he invited them to the stag dance of the dictionary? Should there still be a wedding in the offing?

Stag parties are the most flexible of all the occasions concerned with a wedding, but, nonetheless, they can be tricky affairs. Guests should be particularly careful of what they say about the bride-to-be. Under no circumstances should anyone be allowed to besmirch her name in any way, no matter how tight they get.

Silly remarks about the bride-to-be's virtue or anatomy should never be made. Many a marriage has been ruined before it started because of some stupid remark made about the bride-to-be at a stag party.

Some stag parties are simply men-only dinner parties with speeches, of which what follow are examples. They should be delivered in a lighthearted manner until almost the end.

Stag Party speech No 1

This is almost the last night Jack will be a bachelor. What possessed him to become engaged I don't know. But how Jill has stuck him this far is also beyond me.

Maybe they've heard that two can live as cheaply as one. Well, Christmas is about the only time when this is true. Married people have an advantage then – the two can give as cheaply as one. For the rest of the year the theory that two can live as cheaply as one is nonsense.

Jack perhaps doubts this. If he does, I suggest that on his honeymoon he takes a pound bus ride. He'll find it will cost him two.

There's one piece of advice I want to give him tonight. It is that he makes the best of his honeymoon. It will be his last vacation before taking on a new boss.

Don't think I've got anything against Jill. I think she's a fine girl, and no doubt she'll make Jack a wonderful wife. But marriage won't be so wonderful for her either; she's exchanging the attention of all the men she knows for the *in*attention of Jack.

I hope that Jack's satisfied with Jill's conversation now, and that he'll continue to be satisfied with it until his old age, for I'm told that everything else in marriage is transitory.

Marriage, however, has one definite advantage: Jack won't ever again make a fool of himself without being told about it!

Perhaps Jack is tired of his bachelor life – just one undarned thing after another.

But I'm afraid that nothing short of a miracle will save him now. And you don't hear about many miracles being performed these days, do you? Indeed, some people have difficulty in understanding what they are, even. One of these was an Irishman named Patrick whose priest had spent a long time trying to explain to him what one was. Patrick, however, was still not satisfied. 'Could Your Reverence,' he asked, 'please give me an example of a miracle?'

The priest thought for a moment, then said, 'Yes, Patrick. Turn round, will you?'

Patrick turned round and, as he did so, the priest aimed a fearful kick at his behind.

'Did you feel that?' he asked.

'Sure, I did!' snarled Patrick.

'Well,' said the priest, 'it would have been a miracle if you hadn't.'

Poor old Jack. I've kicked him pretty hard tonight. My conscience is at last starting to trouble me. I confess that I kicked him from purely selfish motives. You see, I'm afraid that, when he's married, I won't be seeing as much of him as I have in the past; that his domestic bliss will be domestic detention, and that for some considerable time ahead we'll have to enjoy ourselves without him.

I wish him the best of good luck. May his marriage be a wonderful success. I ask you to drink to that.

At other stag parties, entertainment is provided – sometimes by professionals, sometimes by friends who do a turn, and sometimes by both.

In every case you must appoint a chairman and you should do this weeks in advance of the event. It is a good plan to ask your best man to be the chairman, except when you have a friend who has experience in organising such entertainment. He will know whom to ask for items for your programme, and a programme you must have. It is imperative that you arrange this in close collaboration with your chairman.

The entertainers should be seen days before your stag party so that your chairman will know exactly what to expect of them, and they will know what they may count on from him. If these are amateur entertainers, then the chairman would be very wise to let them know what time has been allocated to each item. A limit of seven minutes is about right. Audiences are ready for a change after seven minutes and get restless. Many evenings have been marred by one artiste falling in love with the mike – and hogging it.

Should an item take less than seven minutes, all well and good. If he has come across very well he can then be asked to give a second item later in the programme – a possibility of which the chairman should warn the artistes when he tells them that there is a seven-minute limit on all the items.

The concert party may have its own compère. If it has, the chairman should let him take over as soon as he has introduced it, with a very short speech such as this.

Stag Party speech No 2 (Introduction of artistes)

Gentlemen,

During the Victorian era children were told they should be seen and not heard, and that, once I've introduced our splendid entertainers, whom I know you're going to enjoy immensely, will be my role.

But before I sit down, may I say that I have arranged that between items there will be suitable breaks for you to order drinks. This will give our friends the quiet they deserve. Please give it to them.

Gentlemen, it gives me great pleasure to present to you The Staggering Stag Show.

At the end of the show, the chairman should continue with...

Stag Party speech No 3

Gentlemen,

Before we go our various ways, I'm sure you would wish me to thank our good friends for the excellent entertainment they've given us this evening. Your loud and frequent applause has been very convincing evidence of your enjoyment and appreciation. Thank you very much, Gentlemen, for such splendid fare, for which my friends and I now, once again, show our appreciation. *[Applause]*

The other kind of stag party is by far the most frequent.

For this the stags gather at some hostelry at which arrangements for some privacy have been made with the landlord...and much drinking is done.

Again, it is wise to appoint a chairman, and for this we again recommend the best man. At such functions the best, fairest and most agreeable plan is to have a kitty, and guests should be given an estimate of what this might cost them before they come. At the party the chairman will be the toastmaster and could set the ball rolling with this.

Stag Party speech No 4

Gentlemen,

Now that your glasses are charged, let us start formally by drinking to the health and happiness of Jack. God bless the old rascal, and his bride-to-be, too.

Well, that's the end of the formalities, and we can start on the stories.

Soon Jack is to have a mother-in-law. A mother-in-law is a formidable animal, and many a man would love to be in the boots of the young gentleman who, while driving his wife to the shops, was involved in an accident in which, unfortunately, her face got severely injured, and was afterwards very badly scarred.

In due course, they found a plastic surgeon who guaranteed he could do a skin graft that would restore her to her former beauty. There were, however, snags: it would cost them £2000 and he would have to take the skin for the graft from the husband's behind.

They readily agreed to this, and a few months later the young wife was as beautiful as nature intended her to be, so her grateful happy husband put his money in an envelope and took it to the plastic surgeon, smiling all over his face.

The plastic surgeon opened the envelope, counted the money and said, 'You've made a mistake, haven't you? My fee was £2000. There's £3000 here.'

'Oh no I haven't,' said the husband: 'the extra money is for the pleasure I get every time my mother-in-law embraces my wife and kisses my behind.'

While you're thinking of one to cap that, I'll give you another. This one's about friends, like us.

There was a man who arrived in the pub and he was leading a snake on a string.

The landlord didn't like this at all but civilly enough asked, 'Is that snake poisonous?'

'Yes,' said the customer.

'Well, if it bites someone, what happens then?'

'No bother: you just get a friend to suck the poison out of the wound.'

'Supposing,' said the landlord, 'that he bites my behind?'

'Then you'll get to know who your real friends are, won't you?'

[And so on, *ad infinitum....!*]

10

Silver and Gold

At a silver wedding celebration the husband and wife are still sufficiently young for fun. The speech that follows is a mixture of the light-hearted and the serious. It should suit the occasion ideally.

The speech

There are many stories about marriage. The vast majority of them skit at it as an arrangement heavily loaded in favour of women. You know the sort of thing:

'A good husband is one who'll wash up when asked and dry up when told.'

'In marriage, it only takes one to create an argument – your wife!'

'Every time you argue with your wife, words flail you.'

'Marriage is a bargain... Er...someone gets the worse of every bargain!'

If anyone wonders whether such remarks are true, I suggest they should perhaps come to a party such as this.

Any couple who have been married twenty-five years will tell you that the secret of being happily married is to be as polite and considerate to one another as you are to your best friends. The word to use above all others in your relationship together is 'ours'.

John and Mary Smith, whose silver wedding we are tonight celebrating, will, I am sure, endorse this.

Twenty-five years is a long period of time. If it

were possible to confront John and Mary with themselves as they were twenty-five years ago, would they, I wonder, recognise each other? Physically, they doubtlessly would. But I venture to suggest that their personalities have changed unbelievably. Each has taken something from the other. Each has *given* something to the other. They've become almost as one. And each no doubt has improved as a result.

We congratulate them on reaching their silver wedding. That is no small achievement in this day and age. We look forward to the day when they'll be celebrating their *golden* wedding.

And now, the toast: 'Health and many years of happiness to John and Mary Smith'.

At a golden wedding everybody can be as sentimental as they like. There may be present children, grandchildren and perhaps great-grandchildren of the couple who are celebrating their golden wedding.

The speech that follows should be just right for the occasion.

The speech

Today, we are celebrating an event that is becoming rarer and rarer in society. Fifty years of married life is no small achievement. Indeed, fifty years at any job is, these days, a record. And marriage *is* a job, which has to be worked at, as those who try it soon learn. John and Mary Smith have worked so well at it, giving and taking, loving and being loved, that they have become parts of an indivisible whole.

Fifty years ago, John and Mary were young people, full of fun and vigour, laughing at the prospect of married life. I wonder what sort of jokes people were making about marriage in the days when John and

Mary became part of that holy estate.

'The chain of wedlock is so heavy that it takes two to carry it' perhaps?

Or 'In every home there are two ingredients for the perfect murder – a husband and a wife'?

Another one is, 'Why keep another man's daughter?' Or, 'Yawning is a device of nature to enable husbands to open their mouths.'

I suppose the jokes were really pretty much then what they are now.

In fifty years of married life, John and Mary will have heard them all, will have repeated them to each other and will have laughed at them together.

The other day I overheard a man being asked what he would like to be if there were such a thing as reincarnation, and he returned to earth after death.

'Oh,' he said promptly, 'I'd like to be my wife's second husband.'

I'm sure that would be the ambition of John and Mary too, if they ever had a second span of life.

John and Mary must be very proud of one another today. Their family must be delighted with them. Already I'm sure the reminiscences are being exchanged. This is an occasion for sentiment and congratulations.

I feel honoured that the privilege of proposing a toast to two such charming people as John and Mary has been bestowed upon me.

May God spare them for many more years to be a joy to their family, friends and neighbours.

Ladies and gentlemen, will you please join me in drinking a toast, 'To John and Mary – and God bless them both!'

11
Tots and Teens

Christening parties are not occasions for stylised speeches. They are intimate occasions at which one might be called upon to say a few words. What follows should be ample.

The imaginary baby is a boy, and we've given him the names John Paul.

The speech

The other day a little boy was quizzing his mother.

'You say the stork brings babies?' he asked.

'Yes,' said his mother.

'And the Lord gives us our daily bread?'

'Yes, dear!'

'And Santa Claus brings us presents?'

'Yes...!'

'Well, then,' the little boy frowned, 'why do we have to have Daddy?'

I could tell that little boy why we have to have a Daddy. We have to have one to attend parties such as this! Without a Daddy here, this party would scarcely be proper!

No matter what that little boy felt we are glad to have this Daddy around. We congratulate both Jill and him on their lovely baby. I'm sure that he will bring them great joy and happiness. In him they will live on.

Someone has said that a baby is an alimentary canal with a loud voice at one end and no responsibility at the other.

Jack and Jill quite agree that both ends must

function, but how they wish that the times at which they did were more convenient!

We wish this wonder of theirs, whom we heard today christened John Paul, every blessing.

We wish him health. We wish him wealth.
We wish him gold in store.
We wish him heaven when he goes.
Who could wish him more?

An eighteenth birthday party is an occasion for fun, not long speeches.

Frequently someone presents the lucky person whose birthday it is with a golden key. If there is to be but one speech at the party, then the key should be presented at its end. If you use the speech given below you should then alter the last paragraph to read, 'In presenting him with this golden key we wish him health, wealth and happiness all the days of his life.'

Speech No 1

Ladies and gentlemen,

'Old age is honourable.' That is a remark we sometimes hear. But the most wonderful age of all must be eighteen. It's the one birthday we all look forward to. The birthday we acknowledge. Later on some people like to have their birthdays remembered, but not their ages.

Men sometimes take a day off for their birthday. Women, however, are often accused of taking off at least a year. This is really rather foolish, for all you have to do to find any woman's age is to ask her sister-in-law!

The other day I heard about a woman being subpoenaed to give evidence. Before she started, the clerk of the court explained to her that she was only to speak of what she saw, smelled or did. She must not give hearsay evidence; that is, she must not speak of what she was *told*, unless it was told to her by, or in the presence of, the accused. The clerk then nodded to the prosecuting solicitor to begin.

'Madam,' began that worthy, 'what is your age?'

She stared at him for a moment, then smiled blandly before answering, 'I'm not allowed to give hearsay evidence.'

But Gareth has not got to take hearsay evidence of his birthday. There are plenty around who remember it, chief of whom are, of course, his mother and father. They must both be particularly proud today. Proud because, from now on, there's another in their family who enjoys all the privileges of full citizenship, and can now start paying rent!

We congratulate them and we congratulate Gareth, too. We wish him health, wealth and happiness. May he have them all the days of his life.

Speech No 2

You know that I can't make a speech. It's not me at all! But this little verse says all that I want to say.

> *Birthdays are like stepping-stones*
> *Along the path of years;*
> *Here's hoping you will always find,*
> *As each new one appears*
> *That it's a stepping stone as well*
> *To joys and pleasures new,*
> *To still more happy hopes fulfilled*
> *And still more dreams come true.*

Let's drink to that.

12

Other Occasions

Introducing a speaker
Introducing a speaker means that and no more. You should give your audience a brief synopsis of his or her career, qualifications and achievements, emphasising his or her importance in relation to your organisation or audience.

The speech

The next person I shall ask to speak is the lady who represents us at the Palace of Westminster. There she helps to make our laws. She is our representative there – yours and mine – no matter how we voted at the last General Election.

My hope, and hers, is that we did vote – each of us. We owe that to the past – to all those who lived their lives, and even sacrificed them, so that we might have this vote in the government of our land.

Actually, I'm a little sorry for her, for she's seldom able to do full justice to any public dinner. You see, she's always haunted by the knowledge that she might be called upon to make a speech. This is, I suppose, what's known as an occupational hazard.

Having been chairman of this council for twelve months, I have some idea of what this does to her enjoyment of an evening, and sympathise deeply with her.

But, even so, I can't let her off. It would be wrong of me to do so. And most of you would rightly find fault with me.

Well, she really needs no introduction from me.

You must all know her at least by sight. Some of you will have consulted her and enlisted her aid at one of those very helpful surgeries she holds on most Saturday mornings.

She's always a willing listener to everything that we have to say, and ever a tireless worker on our behalf.

It gives me great pleasure to call upon our Member of Parliament, [*name*], to address you.

Welcome!

When you deliver a welcome speech, try to look happy.

After reading the following speeches you should have no difficulty in producing one when you have to welcome people or events.

Welcome speech No 1

I wonder if anyone here actually knows what my job is here this evening? I am here in three roles. First, I'm Chairman of the council. Second, I'm here as your President, and third I am here as Temporary, Acting, Unpaid Chairman of the Local Association – known to all Scouts as the Local Ass.

My job this evening is to welcome you, one and all. I hope that you will all have an excellent time with no embarrassing moments.

Recently, a certain county council gave a dinner in honour of a newly appointed officer. For the sake of anonymity we will call him Mr Smith-Jones. Now we in Anglesey sent a representative to this function. Unfortunately, he had never clapped eyes on Mr Smith-Jones. When he did, he turned to the strange lady who sat on his right and said, 'If that is Mr Smith-Jones, I'm terribly disappointed. I expected him to be far more imposing and intelligent-looking.'

The lady stiffened. 'I beg your pardon,' she said. 'That is Mr Smith-Jones...and do you know who I am?'

Our man shook his head.

'I am *Mrs* Smith-Jones.'

For a moment or two our man was dumbstruck, but presently he recovered himself sufficiently to ask, 'Do you know who *I* am?'

'I do not,' she answered haughtily.

'Well thank God for that,' said he, getting up to leave.

But his experience was not half so bad as that of a young lady who, because she had a touch of hay fever, took two handkerchiefs with her to a dinner party, one of which she tucked in her bosom.

At dinner she began rummaging to the right and to the left in her bosom for the fresh handkerchief. Engrossed in her search, she suddenly realised that conversation had ceased and people were watching her, fascinated. In confusion she murmured, 'I know I had two when I came in.'

A frequent cause of embarrassment at dinner parties is the practice of calling upon someone for a speech without giving him previous warning. That man's plight is often the same as that of the mosquito who arrived at a nudist camp, surveyed the territory and said, 'I don't know where to begin.'

Actually, every man or woman who has to make a speech has my sympathy, for, unaccustomed as I am to public speaking, I know the futility of it.

During my year of office I've had the pleasure of boring many an audience. I've always ignored that doubtlessly excellent advice to all *other* speakers: 'If you don't strike oil in the first three minutes, stop boring.'

Mind you, there have been two or three impolite

characters who have objected. This is how they did so.

'You know, old man, almost every after-dinner speech has a happy ending: everyone's glad when it's over.'

'Er...! Good speeches are like pie. They're better with plenty of shortening.'

'Dear boy, I always think a speech is like a bad tooth: the longer it takes to draw it out, the more it hurts.'

Of course, during my year of office I have had to listen to several speeches too.

One thing soon became evident. The jawbone of an ass is just as dangerous today as in the time of Samson.

Unfortunately, too many speakers confuse the sitting capacity of their audience with the seating capacity of the dining-room.

I wish more speakers would realise that a good speech consists of a beginning and a conclusion, placed not too far apart.

If they did, fewer people would liken a speech to the horns of a steer: a point here and a point there with a great deal of bull in between.

The points I had to make? Well, welcome everybody. Be happy, all of you. Enjoy yourselves, one and all.

Welcome speech No 2

'Me, learn how to paint? Me, learn to take snaps like in the magazines? Never! It's not in me! I never heard such nonsense!!!'

That is an attitude we're all familiar with, isn't it? It is why it gives me so much pleasure to welcome the County Art and Photographic Exhibition to Holyhead once again.

This exhibition will, far more than anything else, help to dispel preconceived prejudices about artistic talent.

Last year the response from the citizens of Holyhead was very good. I hope that this year it will be even better.

Please tell your friends to come along. I'm sure everybody will find something here to interest them. The more who come, the more important in the life of our town will this exhibition be.

The general public in this generation are showing far greater interest and appreciation in matters that concern the arts than ever before. Indeed, not so long ago, the only art exhibitions Holyhead ever got were those provided by the old pavement artists. And what specimens they were! No one could be blamed for mistaking these derelict human beings for tramps.

I remember one who was particularly unprepossessing. He'd drawn a picture of a £5 note and put his upturned cap, in which there were a few coppers, next to it. Beneath, he had written, 'Drawn entirely from memory.'

Today we're accustomed to hearing the word 'culture' on the lips of all sorts of people, and in all kinds of places. To be a cultured person is important, no matter what your walk in life; for culture, you know, is the sum of all the many forms of art, of all constructive thought, and of love.

These, in the course of centuries, have enabled humankind to be less enslaved. They raise us above the level of the animal far more than anything else.

I hope that many who visit this exhibition will be prompted to have a go at something similar to the exhibits that are on display. I can assure those who do that they are on the threshold of discovering a new facet of themselves, and an invaluable sanctuary from the cares and troubles of this mundane humdrum life.

Actually, the goal doesn't matter as much as the road, and all that one experiences on the way.

In the hope that some of the citizens of Holyhead may, as a result of this exhibition, discover this fact for themselves, I am very glad to welcome it to our town.

Thank you and goodbye
At the end of a conference or activity week it is often the practice to round off with a general get-together of all the delegates and/or participants for a closing – down session. The following speech is the sort of thing that's called for on such occasions.

The speech

When I welcomed you at the beginning of the week I immediately tried to put you out of your misery by telling you that I was not a lengthy speaker.

Even so, I must tell you what Lord Mancroft had to say about this.

'A speech,' he said, 'is like a love affair. Any fool can start it, but to end it requires considerable skill.'

I'll keep that in mind for the next few moments, and hope that you will afterwards say that his words fell on good ground.

This evening, however, I do want to say how much I personally have enjoyed having you here.

During the week we have met on several occasions; occasions which I myself have thoroughly enjoyed.

I'd like to say thank you to all of you for your courtesy and pleasant greetings whenever we met. I want to say thank you, too, to members of our Sailing

Club for their kindness and hospitality. I hope that praise from me, a non-sailor, for all the splendid work they've evidently put in, in connection with this week's activities, will not seem out of place.

At the beginning of the week I told you that we were proud of our sailing facilities. I repeat this tonight, but with far greater conviction, for I have since been taken out on a catamaran to watch you racing. Some of the mysteries of your exciting sport were then explained to me, and indeed I sampled a thrill or two.

We know that people who have once been here want to come again. I sincerely hope that this is your experience and that you will visit us regularly.

We have nothing to hide here. I remember hearing a story many years ago about a very respectable citizen who had one secret, which he wished to keep from everyone. It was that his father had been hanged for murder. He was very successful in concealing this information from all his friends and acquaintances and was a model citizen in every respect.

One day, however, like all other thoughtful people, he decided to take out an insurance policy and was given a long application form to fill in. One question, however, rather took him aback. It was, 'Are your parents alive? If not, state cause of death.'

He got out of this quandary by putting down: 'My mother died of pneumonia at 89 and my father was taking part in an official function when the platform unfortunately gave way.'

We have no secrets here and we have plenty of sources of enjoyment for people who like the sea and country.

Come and explore our country and you'll find that time will fly. Time, after all, is relative and months can seem like hours and days can fly like minutes.

I remember hearing about a man who was given six months to live by his doctor. He was very distressed by this and asked, 'Is there anything I can do, doctor?'

The doctor replied, 'Do you smoke?'

'Yes,' said the man.

'Cut it out,' said the doctor. 'Do you drink?'

'Yes,' said the man.

'Cut it out,' said the doctor. 'Do you go out with young ladies?'

'Yes,' said the man.

'Cut it out,' said the doctor.

'Well,' said the man glumly, 'if I do all these things will I live longer than six months?'

'No,' said the doctor. 'But it'll *seem* much longer.'

I hope that you've all enjoyed yourselves so much that your time here has flown and that you now feel that you must come again.

13

Raise Your Glasses –
Toasts and Responses

At the conclusion of each of the three speeches that follow, there is a toast.

The first is to the coxswain, crew and helpers of the Holyhead branch of the National Lifeboat Association. This being such an important body in the life of the port of Holyhead, it was considered proper that their toast should be proposed by the town's first citizen. The second is spoken by the president of the Scouts' Local Association, again in Holyhead.

The third speech can be used for almost any occasion without adaptation.

Toast speech No 1

If I were asked to name the dinners that I feel it an honour to attend, I would put yours, this evening, very high on the list. I consider it an even greater honour to be asked to address the annual dinner of this institution which plays such a vital part in the life of our town.

Members of the lifeboat crew are men of action who, I know, will have little patience with long speeches.

It has been said that a speech is like a bad tooth: the longer it takes to draw out, the more the thing hurts.

Well, I certainly don't want to hurt you in any way this evening. I have no intention of making a long, drawn-out speech. But it would be churlish of me if I were to let this opportunity pass without saying how very proud we are of you and your record.

Most institutions come in for criticism by the general public. I am a member of the district council and the county council, and I can assure you that people really enjoy criticising those two institutions!

That is democracy, I suppose. They elect you so that they can pull you to pieces for the next few years.

But I have never heard a single word of criticism of our Lifeboat.

We landlubbers stand in awe of the power and might of the oceans. Indeed, a rough crossing to Ireland incapacitates the majority of us, and we think of the sea as the *cruel* sea. In consequence, we have nothing but admiration for people like you, who are prepared to pit their skill and strength against stormy and tempestuous seas for the purpose of saving life.

I remember hearing about a young man who entered a monastery hoping to become a monk. The order that he wished to join had a strict rule of silence. The abbot told him on his first day that he would be on probation for fifteen years. During that time he would be allowed to speak only once every five years, and then only for one minute with the abbot himself.

The young man accepted and was registered as a novitiate.

Eventually, the first five years passed and he was summoned to the abbot's study.

'How are you going on, my son?' asked the abbot.

'Oh, all right, thank you, Reverend Father,' replied the young man.

'Have you any complaints?' asked the abbot.

'Well, sir, yes, there is one thing...the porridge is always cold at breakfast. It would be so much nicer if it were hot.'

'Right,' said the abbot, 'I will see to that. Time is now up.'

The young man left and didn't speak again to anyone for five years. Then he had to go again to the abbot's study.

'How are you going on?' asked the abbot.

'Oh, all right, thank you, sir, I think,' answered the novitiate.

'Have you any complaints?' asked the abbot.

'Well, sir, there is just one thing: the bed's very hard and I find it difficult to sleep. Could I please have a little more straw in my palliasse?'

'Right,' said the abbot, 'I will see to that. Time is now up.'

And the young man had to leave.

Another five years passed and the young man went to see the abbot for the last time.

'Reverend Father,' he said, 'my fifteen years' probation is at an end. Are you going to accept me as a full member of your order?'

'Dear me, no,' replied the abbot. 'You've done nothing but complain since you came here!'

Well, we don't complain about the lifeboat people, even once in five years, and I'm happy to pay you the highest tribute this evening. You maintain a high and honourable standard and live up to a noble tradition.

I remember hearing about two soldiers who had to walk all the way from Criccieth to Bangor. It was summer and the day was particularly hot.

After they'd walked many miles they saw a woman standing in the garden of her cottage.

'How many miles is it to Bangor?' asked one of the soldiers.

'Oh, about ten,' replied the woman.

They continued walking for another hour and then

they met a shepherd.

'How many miles is it to Bangor?' asked the soldier again.

'Oh, about ten,' answered the shepherd.

Feeling very hot and very tired, they trudged on for another half-hour. Then they met a schoolboy.

'How many miles are we from Bangor, son?' asked the same soldier.

'About ten, I think,' answered the boy.

The soldier turned to his companion and, with a cynical smile, remarked, 'Well, mate, we're at least holding our own.'

The Holyhead Lifeboat always holds its own and always maintains its high tradition.

It gives me the greatest pleasure to propose the toast to: 'The Coxswain, Crew and Helpers of the Holyhead branch of the National Lifeboat Association'.

Toast speech No 2

The Scout movement commands a very warm place in my heart. Always when I think of it, I do so with pleasure and gratitude. Pleasure, because, again and again, I savour cherished scouting memories. Gratitude, because the movement gave me some of the happiest hours of my life. It brought me into contact with some excellent people of all ages whom I would otherwise never have met.

I am not going to show my gratitude by inflicting a very long speech on you. If I did, some of you would afterwards be reminding me of that ancient proverb, 'Gratitude is the least of the virtues and ingratitude is the worst of vices.'

It is an odd thing, but we human beings are much

more interested in the vices of our fellows than in their virtues. Perhaps because of this we tend sometimes to get wrong notions about one another.

One of the oldest maxims among newspaper people is that evil is news, goodness commonplace. They naturally exploit this. That is why so many newspapers are full of evil and prophecies of evil things to come.

Now listen to this evil thing:

'Corruption, vice and laxity are the rule today. And this is particularly true of our youth. Our society cannot carry on, for the young men of our nation are given up to vain, useless pleasures. They think not at all about tomorrow. They live in foolishness – just for today. Woe, woe to our country, and land of our fathers!'

What do you think of that? Typical of the newspapers, isn't it? Isn't that what we are hearing and reading everywhere today? This is the gloomy and despondent view too many people have today regarding the future.

But take heart! Those words were not taken from any newspaper. On the contrary, they were spoken two thousand five hundred years before the birth of Jesus by King Urukagina of Sumeria.

Don't let such unkind remarks, such prophecies, ever depress you. Throughout all the centuries which have passed since King Urukagina was alive, some people have always enjoyed being prophets of doom. They were saying something similar when I was a boy. Yes, and such things as, 'Spare the rod and spoil the child... In real old age, children are a great comfort, and they help you to reach it much quicker, too.'

If people were only to reflect for a few moments on what they are about to say before uttering such damaging things about youth they would realise that it is not so much the youth of the ages that are to blame for the corruption, vice and laxity, but those who have reached the so-called age of discretion and responsibility.

Some of us who remember the Seventies probably know someone who was a punk, whether it's a friend, relative or neighbour. Even if we don't know one personally, we used to see them in the high street on a Saturday afternoon.

When they first appeared on the scene, people wondered why they did it. Why should they want to look so odd and completely different from the rest of the population? Was it to protest against something? Was it to make their parents angry?

Perhaps these factors did play a part in their decision to wear such extravagant dress. But I believe they were really expressing a fundamental struggle to be different from those older generations. They just wanted to do things differently.

People getting on in years will tell you that it's unwise to cast aside the customs and traditions of centuries. Some of them, they will agree, perhaps need modifying, but *casting aside?* Dear me, no! These people maintain that our customs and traditions are the result of the experience of many generations.

Personally, I find that age improves wine, compound interest and little else!

Solomon, you know, first wrote the *Song of Songs* – a beautiful thing about love; then he wrote *Proverbs,* parts of which are always being quoted at you; lastly he wrote *Ecclesiastes,* which, to put it mildly, is a cynical book. But that is the way of humankind in this world. When we are young we compose songs and write poetry; then later we take to making sententious remarks; and lastly, when we're old, we speak of the vanity of things.

But you in the Scout movement are not concerned with the vanity of things. You go about doing things that are constructive, useful. You can change the world. And it *would* change, too, if every Scout, every Scouter, every Guide and every Guider did their best to obey the law of their movements:

> *Trusty, Loyal, Helpful,*
> *Brotherly, Courteous, Kind,*
> *Obedient, Smiling, Thrifty,*
> *Pure as the rustling wind.*

That short verse contains all the tenets of your law. Obey it and you will make the world a better, happier, more godly place. If you live up to your law you will make a far greater, far more lasting change than any of those modern cults which are forever being created – and forgotten! The challenge is with you.

In the hope that you will, each of you, henceforth remember this, I give you the most important toast of the evening: 'Scouting!'

Toast speech No 3

'Judge not, that ye be not judged!' I find those words most appropriate this evening.

My toast is that of 'Our Guests'. If I make a porridge of it, I advise the lady who has to reply that to tell me so would be a breach of etiquette. And for anyone else who may be inclined to criticise I quote Sir Francis Bacon: 'In revenge, haste is criminal!' Who knows how long it will be before you will be standing, uncomfortably, where I am?'

I hope that all this has softened your hearts, put you

in a mood to sympathise with me and approve of the little I have to say to you tonight.

I am very glad to welcome our guests, although gladness and public speaking don't somehow go together with me.

When we entertain we try to be sociable, we bring out the nicest part of our nature. The more we do this, the pleasanter people will find us. This old world of ours will consequently seem a brighter place to them.

We hope that you are enjoying yourselves with us and making friends. I like Abraham Lincoln's definition of a friend. Try it on whoever is sitting next to you – not while I'm speaking, of course! Lincoln said that a friend is someone who has the same enemies as yourself.

Speaking of enemies, and seeing quite a few bottles around, reminds me of an experience a friend of mine who enjoyed his wine had recently. The minister of his wife's church, who was a hellfire, temperance man, called on him one day to remonstrate with him about his occasional alcoholic indiscretions. 'Drink,' he said to my friend, 'drink is your greatest enemy.'

My friend smiled indulgently at him and retorted, 'But padre, doesn't holy writ instruct us to love our enemies?'

Staying on the subject of religion and sermons, I heard the other day about three small boys who were bragging about their fathers.

'My father,' said the first, 'writes a few short lines on a piece of paper and calls it a poem, then he sends it away and gets fifty pounds for it.'

'Huh!' snorted the second little boy. 'My father puts dots on a piece of paper and calls it a song and then he sends it away and gets five hundred pounds for it.'

'Bah!' exclaimed the third little boy. 'That's nothing. My father writes a sermon on a piece of paper, goes into the pulpit to read it and it takes six men to carry in the money.'

There's a great deal to be said for a good sermon. It helps people in several ways. Some rise from it strengthened. Others awake from it refreshed.

You can say this of speeches, too.

I don't expect my speech tonight to have strengthened anybody. On the other hand, nobody has gone to sleep, either. That really is not at all bad, you know. Give me a moment or two and I'll prove to you that I'm a 'finished' speaker – I'll sit down.

But before I do so I must thank our guests for accepting our invitation. Thank you for being our guests; we are very glad you came.

You other ladies and gentlemen who are here – thank you for giving me your attention. I ask but one thing more of you, that you rise and drink the toast of 'Our Guests', coupled with the name of Mrs [*name of special guest*].

In the two speeches that follow we see what may be typical *replies* to the toast of 'Our Guests'. The occasions in these examples are a British Legion dinner and a sailing club dinner.

With very little effort, you can change a speech prepared as a *reply* to the toast of 'Our Guests' to one of *proposing* the toast, and vice versa.

Reply speech No 1

'Do you know what is harder to bear than the reverses of fortune?' is a question once asked by that great soldier, Napoleon Bonaparte. He answered it himself with these words: 'It is the baseness, the hideous ingratitude of man.'

Well, I'm going to make quite sure that you guests this evening are not accused of ingratitude by starting my speech with saying thank you very much for inviting us here tonight. We are thoroughly enjoying ourselves.

To the gentleman who so ably proposed this toast, may I say a special thank you. My fellow guests and I are most grateful to you, sir [*or Mr Johnson, Miss Evans, or even Bill or Pauline, depending on how familiar you and fellow guests are with your hosts*], for your kind words.

When I decided to come here this evening I sought information about the British Legion. I discovered that it was founded by Earl Haig in 1921 to serve the interests of ex-servicemen.

First of all, you, its members, served your country, and now you band yourselves together to serve one another.

Your kind has been honoured throughout the centuries.

This evening I pay you my tribute, recalling, as I do so, the words of Robert Louis Stevenson... 'So long as we love, we serve. So long as we are loved by others, we are indispensable; and no man's useless while he has a friend.'

You serve one another. You are true friends. And the only way to have a true friend is to *be* a true friend.

Now most of you will, I'm sure, agree that in the services one of the most helpful and friendly people is the padre.

One of these was, during the First World War, trying to console a young soldier in the trenches who was trembling with fright.

'Look,' he said, 'stop worrying. If a bullet has got

your name on it, you'll get it come what may. And if it hasn't got your name on it you won't get it, and you've wasted all this energy worrying over nothing.'

The young soldier thought about this for some moments, and then turned to the padre. 'You're right, padre,' he said. 'If a bullet's got my name on it I'm bound to get it whether I worry or not, and I'll take your word for it that those that have some other name on them are not intended for me. But what worries me is those that come over with nothing on them but, "To whom it may concern"!'

In war, as in all 'far' distant events, we don't really know what exactly happened, and have to depend on correspondents for information.

In the Falklands and Gulf wars, our armed forces wrote more pages of glory for the annals of our beloved country, manifesting bravery unsurpassed and exhibiting loyalty with patriotism of the highest order.

Many are the stories we have heard and read of our most worthy armed forces. Its members lived up to the highest traditions of our great fighting services. They deserve all honour and glory.

However, one of the stories that came to my mind is about a war correspondent.

This particular war correspondent was a cook on board an aircraft carrier and was at the time well away from the fighting zone.

He had just finished frying masses of eggs for his shipmates. Tired and weary, he took up his pen and sat down to write a letter to his sweetheart.

'Dearest Girl,' he wrote, 'for the past three hours shells have been bursting all round me.'

Which, of course, was true!

After war, we need benevolence, charity on all sides. Instead, we get political expedients. Too often the negotiators are politicians, not statesmen. They think about the next election, not the next generation.

That little boy who was sent to church by his father with a £1 coin and a £5 note in his pocket will make a good politician when he grows up.

'You are to put whichever you please on the collecting plate,' said his father. 'Listen to the sermon and decide whether to give £1 or £5 in accordance with the impression that it makes on you.'

When the little boy returned from church his father asked him which he had put on the plate: £5 or £1.

'Oh, £1,' said the boy. 'I was going to give £5, then I remembered what the preacher had said in his sermon...'

'What was that?' interrupted his father.

'The Lord loves a *cheerful* giver!'

But benevolence is not always appreciated. I'm sure that, from time to time, you have all found this out. Indeed, it was only the other day that I was told about an ageing lady who had all through her life practised benevolence. She had been a munificent supporter of many worthy causes. But this did not always please her family.

One day her smart-Alec nephew jibed, 'Oh, Auntie, you must be on the suckers list of practically every charity that was ever thought of.'

'My dear,' she replied, 'I don't mind that at all, provided you spell it s-u-c-c-o-u-r.'

Succour, too, is, I suppose, something you all now need – succour from me and my speech. Thank you for listening to me. I wish all of you and your splendid Legion every success.

Reply speech No 2

> *Rule, Britannia, Britannia rule the waves;*
> *Britons never will be slaves.*

So sang the poet in the middle of the eighteenth century. And it was people like you, who had spent their spare time messing about with boats, who saved Britons from being slaves in 1940. The enormous contribution of the weekend sailors to the evacuation of our troops stranded at Dunkirk commands an illustrious page in the history of our island.

Sailing is probably the sport with the greatest useful potential of all the sports in which we indulge. It touches on practically everything that the landlubber does, and a great deal more besides. You never know when what you pick up as part-time sailors will be of service to you.

I feel highly honoured at being allowed to join you once more. It is always a pleasure to mix with a group of people as congenial and pleasant as our Sailing Club members.

Speaking of conviviality, I remember hearing of two brothers who were very close to each other. Each evening they would go to the local pub and each would have a double whisky – an excellent fraternal procedure of which I thoroughly approve.

Everyone in the local knew of this daily habit and indeed looked forward to the arrival of the brothers each evening.

One day, however, one of the brothers told them that they wouldn't be seeing him any more for a very long time. He was having to go overseas to work.

The parting was very sad, but the brother who was staying in this country promised he would keep up the old custom and go to the local at the same time each evening. There would, however, be one difference. In future, he would drink two double whiskies instead of one – the second one to be his brother's.

This arrangement went on religiously for many

months, and the regulars became accustomed to seeing the lone brother coming in, ordering two doubles and drinking them.

Then there came a change. The brother came in looking very miserable. Gloomily, he ordered one double whisky and drank it without pleasure. This went on for two or three evenings until at the end of the week the other customers could stand it no more.

'We've noticed,' they said to the lone drinker, 'that you've changed your ways. Nothing's happened to your brother, has it?'

'No, nothing's happened to my brother,' said the man, 'but something's happened to *me*. I've gone teetotal.'

I've told you many times that I don't believe in making lengthy speeches. I am, too, at a disadvantage here in that I'm not really versed in the subject of sailing. It would be useless for me to try to fool experts like you by pretending that I am. Instead, I will tell you about a sailor who went into a public house while he was home on leave. There he met a man with whom he got friendly. Over the drinks they talked, then seemingly in no time the landlord was calling, 'Time, gentlemen, please!'

'Pity,' said the sailor's friend. 'But never mind. What about coming home with me instead?'

The sailor frowned. 'What for?' he asked.

'Oh, some wine, women and song,' smiled his friend.

The sailor smiled back. 'OK,' he said. 'Suits me. All I've had over the past six months is rum, pin-ups and baccy.'

There are, evidently, still privations at sea.

Privations and dangers.

Ships still get wrecked, and sailors are still washed ashore on desert islands. One sailor who had been on an island for two years was delighted one morning to see a ship anchor close to and lower a boat which was rowed towards him. As he grounded on the beach, an officer threw him a bundle of newspapers.

'We saw your signal,' he said, 'but the Captain thinks you ought to read these and then let us know if you still want to be rescued.'

Well one thing seems certain: by now, you will all want to be rescued from me and my speech.

Thank you very much for inviting us as your guests. And thank you, particularly, Mr Vice-Commodore, for the kind things you said about your guests when you proposed the toast to us. I know I am expressing the feelings of each one of us when I say that sailing club people are good company and that it is always a joy to be with them.

We wish you good sailing and fair weather in all your activities.

14

Fraternities

Fraternities usually have a dinner after they have gone through their various ceremonies. At this, people make speeches. The candidate is always welcomed and so are visiting brethren. Specimens of speeches that do this follow, together with one that a candidate could use for his reply.

But before we go to them perhaps a brief account of the two most popular fraternities that follow this routine might be found useful.

I refer to the Rotarians and the Freemasons.

Rotarians started their life in Chicago. They were started by businessmen in 1905 to further business service, foster social relations and encourage high ethical standards in business.

Of the four men who started Rotary International, one was a coal dealer, one a merchant tailor, one a mining operator and another a lawyer.

Freemasonry is a secret society, having lodges for reciprocal assistance and social enjoyment all over the world. Roman Catholics have their own fraternity, which is called the Knights of St Columba.

The Freemasons' Grand Lodge of England was established in 1707; that of Ireland in 1730; and that of Scotland in 1736.

Speech No 1 (welcoming a newly elected brother)

I heard the other day about a man who was sent to work in a strange city. At once he started attending one of its churches. He expected that soon the clergyman or some member of the congregation would come to ask him about himself and try to make him welcome there. But no one ever did.

This disappointed him terribly and indeed he would have left and gone to some other church but for the fact that he liked this one and its services very much. Then he had a brainwave. He tore a £10 note in half. On one half he wrote, 'If the clergyman or any member of this church calls on me I will give him the other half of this note. I have been a regular worshipper at your church for weeks now and would be thankful for a little Christian fellowship from anyone there.'

He added his name and address and the following Sunday put it on the collecting plate.

Of course, the next day the clergyman arrived, full of apologies.

Now you who have become one of us this evening, you will never have an experience like that here.

Here a welcome awaits you always; we believe that friendship can only be bought with friendship. There is an old proverb that runs, 'Go often to the house of thy friend for weeds choke up the unused path.' Do, please, try to attend our meetings regularly. The more we see of you the better we like it and the better we will come to know one another.

We call our members Brothers, a word that you cannot say without, at the same time, using the word Others. Others are important to us in this fraternity, particularly others less fortunate than ourselves. Never, I hope, do we think of brothers in the way of that small boy who went into a shop where they were giving away toy balloons as an advertising gimmick.

'Can I have two, please?' he asked.

'Sorry,' said the manager, 'we can only give one to everyone.'

The little boy's face fell to such an extent that the

manager added, 'But perhaps you have a brother at home?'

Although he wanted that other balloon so very badly, the little boy wouldn't lie. Instead, he said, 'No, sir, but my sister has a brother.'

Well, we have acquired another brother in you tonight. We welcome you sincerely. If new brethren did not come along our organisation would become effete and presently die. It is new blood in the form of newly-elected brethren that keeps us alive and fresh and gives us hope for the future.

That you will be very happy in our midst is the wish of everyone whom you will now see rising and drinking the toast to our newly elected brother.

Brethren, I give you the toast of: 'Our Newly Elected Brother.'

Speech No 2 (the newly elected brother replies)

Standing here in front of you all I remember hearing about a small boy who was looking at a picture of Daniel standing outside the lions' den. 'Daddy,' said the small boy, 'why is Daniel smiling? Any moment now he'll he thrown into the lions' den and so far as he knows that'll be the end of him.'

'Well,' said the father, 'it's probably because he realises that when the feasting is over he won't be called on to say anything.'

Thank you for accepting me as a member of your organisation. As yet I don't know a great deal about it. But what little I have assimilated this evening makes me feel that I am going to enjoy being one of you very much.

I will always strive to live up to the principles of your organisation so that the two kind gentlemen who proposed and seconded me will never feel that in doing so they made a mistake.

To all of you who have welcomed me, I say thank you very much. To you, sir, for the way you proposed this toast, my gratitude.

Speech No 3 (visiting brethren)

'Those friends thou hast and their adoption tried,
Grapple them to thy soul with hoops of steel.'

So spoke the Immortal Bard. And so say we. We are always glad to have friends to visit us. One of the advantages of being a member of a fraternity such as ours is that we have many friends whom we have never seen before. For are not friends those who obey the same code and have the same loyalties, ambitions and interests as ourselves?

No one can become a member of our fraternity without first submitting himself to a strict examination and afterwards going through a ceremony of initiation. From this time onwards a new brother obeys the same code and stands for the same loyalties, ambitions and interests as ourselves – indeed, he is one of us, and the words of William Shakespeare I quoted earlier apply to him.

By visiting one another we get to know our brethren and their ways.

The danger in a fraternity such as ours is that it might become parochial. But visiting brethren bring us news of what takes place at other branches of our fraternity. They bring us new ideas. Discussions with them remind us that our interests should extend beyond the confines of our own town. They prevent us from becoming self-centred. And self-centredness can be a very dangerous thing.

I heard the other day of a very self-centred little

girl. One day she ran into the kitchen and threw herself into her mother's arms.

'Mummy!' she wept. 'Michael's broken my dolly.'

'Oh, what a pity!' consoled her mother. 'How did he manage that?'

'He wouldn't give me one of his sweets,' howled the girl, 'so I hit him over the head with it.'

I suppose that, if I do not sit down fairly soon, someone will take it into his head to hit me on the head with something.

I am very glad to welcome you, our visitors. Do come again. We are delighted to see you. It is with great pleasure that I propose the toast of 'Our Visitors'.

15

Women's Organisations

The speeches that follow are addresses to a Women's Institute branch and a branch of the Union of Townswomen's Guilds.

They will be well received not only because members of these organisations will approve of the fact that you have troubled to find out something about them, but, too, because many members may learn more about their organisation from listening to these addresses than they ever did before.

Speech No 1 (Women's Institute)

The other day a friend of mine produced a very smart, hand-sewn, leather wallet. 'Look at that,' he said. 'My wife made it. Learned how at the Women's Institute.'

I'd always thought that the Women's Institute was a place where ladies got together once in a while for a cup of tea and a chat, and that's all. After my friend's revelation I started making inquiries and what a surprise I've had!

Your organisation is a tremendous force for good in the community. I have discovered that you exist to bring women together to learn things that will be of help in their homes. Also, you endeavour to improve the environment of your neighbourhood.

Every right-thinking person will agree that such objectives are to be commended and should be fostered in every possible way.

You go about it in a more practical fashion at each

of your monthly meetings by dividing them into three parts.

First, you deal with the business of your association: for example, reading the minutes of your last meeting, all of which is carried on, in proper form, by your own members.

Then you have a lecture or a demonstration given by an outside speaker, or perhaps sometimes a short talk by one of your own members. This is how my friend got his excellent wallet.

Last, you have tea. For getting to know one another and making friends, nothing works like a bit to eat and a drink of some sort.

What better methods could anyone conceive to develop in a group a spirit of friendliness, co-operation and initiative?

These three are of the highest importance in any community. You are, I am told, dedicated to developing them among yourselves. Let us take them one by one.

Friendship! I quote that brilliant 17th-century essayist, Joseph Addison: 'Friendship improves happiness and abates misery by doubling our joy and dividing our grief.' How right he was. There's no doubt that friendships improve every community, no matter what its size.

I am glad to say that your faces seem to me to be those of happy people. I am sure that you will readily admit that you owe part of that happiness to your Women's Institute.

Then you aim to develop co-operation among your members. This little story will show you how important co-operation can be.

A few days ago I was talking to a fisherman who told me that he was, at long last, really prospering.

'I'm very glad,' I said. 'What's happened to

improve things?'

'Well,' he said, 'It's like this: I've taken a partner. He's an expert boat-handler so he handles the boat and leaves me alone to do the fishing. That way we catch far more than either of us did alone.'

'Freckles,' said someone, 'would be a nice tan if they got together.'

Last, you aim to develop initiative.

You do not need me to tell you the importance of initiative. It's a word you're constantly hearing, a quality that's praised everywhere today. The more initiative there is in our country, the more sure it is of prospering. I heard a man put it very neatly the other day: 'Develop initiative,' he said, 'for ruts often deepen into graves.'

Not only will you, as members of this great organisation, be better people for developing friendliness, co-operation and initiative, but you will foster them at home to the benefit of your families.

Friendliness, co-operation and initiative in the home soon spread out into the streets. Soon your community finds it is a place of developing friendliness, co-operation and initiative.

And what is Britain but a collection of communities? Your potential power is immense.

I wish you all the good luck possible. Do please enthusiastically carry on the good work.

Speech No 2 (Townswomen's Guilds)

Walter Lippman, an American teacher and editor of stature, said, 'The principles of good society call for a concern with an order of being (which cannot be proved existentially to the sense organs), where it matters supremely that the human person is inviolable, that reason shall regulate the will, that truth shall prevail over error.'

Those words seem to me to encapsulate the aims, and, I would add, ambitions of the Union of Townswomen's Guilds.

I do thank you very much for inviting me to your meeting here today.

I've been telling friends that I was coming, and – do you know? Very few of them know much about you. Probably the best I got was, 'They're the townswomen's answer to the countrywomen's Women's Institutes; but don't sing *Jerusalem*.'

Someone else thought that the Union of Townswomen's Guilds was a society of professional women. None of the men I asked had any idea. Yes, this in spite of the fact that, as the Union of Townswomen's Guilds, you have been established since 1932.

Actually, under other names such as the National Union of Societies for Equal Citizenship and the National Union of Women's Suffrage Societies you have been going since the end of the last century. Such a record deserves congratulations and I hasten to pass mine on to you.

You believe, passionately, in education for women.

Emerson, you will remember, said that 'the things taught in colleges and schools are not an education, but the *means* of an education.'

You are for ever trying to discover new methods of attracting the interest of women in scholarship. You endeavour to intrigue them so that they want to get to know more, with the result that they are led to more continuous study.

Education is found to enhance people's contribution to the common good, thus making them better, more valuable citizens.

Moreover, education makes one fitter company for

oneself as well as for others.

Was it not Aristotle who said, 'Education is an ornament in prosperity and a refuge in adversity'? So you win in all ways.

You hold lectures and endeavour to foster interest in music, drama, handicrafts and civics.

'Music,' mused Carlyle, 'is well said to be the speech of angels' – and who can better that?

Drama? Ah, well, I know a little story about drama. There was this man who said to his friend, who enjoyed the theatre, 'Albert, what's the difference between a drama and a melodrama?'

Albert took a few moments to compose his thoughts, but presently said, 'Well, in a drama the heroine merely throws the villain over. In a melodrama, she throws him over a cliff.'

Handicrafts? I imagine that handicrafts could kindle in you ladies an interest in the do-it-yourself movement. Some say that this do-it-yourself movement is bad for business. Well, everybody is painting his own house and repairing his own furniture. And there are all kinds of facilities to help the do-it-yourself fan to produce a professional job – such as sprays instead of brushes, lambswool rollers and even drip-dry paint!

A neighbour assured me that a chap in our road is making a fortune out of this do-it-yourself business. He goes round repairing do-it-yourself botches! So, ladies, beware!

Your studies of civics show you that every one of us has responsibilities in the community. Prominent among these is our duty to see that homes are built; that families are properly reared; that our sick, needy and suffering are cared for; and that adults, as well as children, are educated.

Further, they show that, as good citizens, we have

the responsibility of seeing that action is taken to eliminate disease, accidents and disasters.

All of this gives us pride in our community, and ourselves.

Meeting here each month, you get to know one another, and make friends. Friendship is the wine of life. It is Heaven that gives us friends to bless the present scene, which I hope will continue to move forward for you in many ways and ever be a joy to you all. Long may you prosper.

God bless you and your very worthwhile endeavours.

16
Youth

The two speeches that follow are addresses to youth clubs. They are not simply social speeches. Each contains a message and is an appeal, for each tries to get the audience to do something that will be to their benefit.

They are included for two reasons. First, because there are today so many youth organisations that one never knows when one might be called upon to address one. Second, because they demonstrate how to address the same group on two separate occasions on two aspects of what is basically the same subject: their welfare, or, if you prefer, their good.

A vicar was recently recalling how, as a young curate, he had been dismayed at the prospect of preparing two sermons for every Sunday throughout his ministry. That, he calculated, meant about five thousand sermons. He would never have enough to say!

Despondently he went to his ageing vicar to ask how *he* had managed. 'Oh,' said the old man. 'It's not so hard, you'll find.'

'But what shall I preach about?' asked the curate.

'God,' said the vicar. 'Just God.'

The popular conception is that addresses about God should be reserved for religious meetings and are inappropriate elsewhere. But add another *o* and *ness* to *God* and you have *Goodness*. You now have a subject of infinite capacity upon which you can make an endless number of speeches.

Speech No 1

I've read in one of our national daily newspapers that the majority of young people who go on protest

121

marches do so for very different reasons from those of the organisers.

Sometimes, as you will no doubt have seen on the television, these marches get rather out of hand, tempers run high and violence is caused both to people and to property.

This newspaper went on to say that most of those people participating in protest marches are only interested in causing trouble.

And that's how it always is, isn't it? The majority of older people seem to think that their function in life is to find fault with the young. Not only finding fault, but misinterpreting practically everything they do.

Why do they do this? Why can't they understand and encourage instead?

Is it because they're jealous of you? Jealous of your youth? Jealous that you have that which they have lost? Could be!

The worst of it is, of course, that you're in the minority. Moreover, that all too soon you may become like them.

Impossible though it may seem to you, they, not so long ago, were like you – full of life, full of enthusiasm, resilient and light-hearted. Your problem is how to avoid degenerating into vegetables like them.

In the case of the majority of men – and this has been so for generations – you could inscribe on their tombstones, 'This man died at thirty. He was buried at seventy.'

You should do your utmost to prevent this tragedy happening to you.

It's easy to say this. Talk is cheap. The problem is, how *can* you avoid degenerating into vegetables? Well, I think you must, above all, convince yourselves that you are worthwhile. And you *are* worthwhile, provided you're working at something. This country of ours is a good country. It is a good country in which to live, both in sickness and in health. I'm not saying it's the ideal country in which to live. There are probably many ways in which it can be improved. That's not the point at the moment. What matters now is that, whatever your work, it matters. It makes you part of the mechanism that keeps this country going.

When you work, use your imagination when thinking about your job, and when you're talking about it to others. I'll tell you a story that illustrates this very well.

When a cathedral was being built, a visitor approached three stonemasons and asked each of them what he was doing. The first man said, 'I'm cutting stones.' The second: 'Earning forty pounds a day.' And the third said proudly, 'I'm building a wonderful new cathedral.'

Try to see your work as an integral part of your community. You'll find that this helps your self-confidence immensely.

This community of ours is one that improves generation after generation. So keep your ideals alive. Never be afraid to discuss them. You never know what seeds you sow in so doing.

Your ideals and ideas are living things that can grow and multiply only when you discuss them with others.

Therefore, take every opportunity to examine them and argue about them publicly.

Remember that you will always be as young as your faith, your self-confidence and hope. There is doubt, fear and despair that make you old and turn you into vegetables.

You may not be given the opportunity to make great changes in anything in the world. Indeed, such power falls to very, very few. And it is just as true to say that very, very few of us really want it.

Shakespeare gave young people some very good advice, you know.

Now, don't let the way *school* served up Shakespeare's work ruin him for you for ever. Turn to him once in a while.

In the peculiar language that he used, you'll find practically every emotion you'll ever experience. Just listen to the verses I'm about to read. It may be your first experience of rejecting a prejudice you've formed; that is always a good thing.

What I'm about to read may cause you to have second thoughts and admit that there is perhaps something in the old boy after all. If you achieve that this evening, then its importance in your life is immeasurable.

With Shakespeare's advice to young people I end.

Look thou character. Give thy thoughts no tongue,
Nor any unproportion'd thought his act.
Be thou familiar, but by no means vulgar;
The friends thou hast, and their adoption tried,
Grapple them to thy soul with hoops of steel;
But do not dull thy palm with entertainment
Of each new-hatch'd unfledg'd comrade. Beware
Of entrance to a quarrel; but, being in,
Bear't, that th'opposed may beware of thee.
Give every man thine ear, but few thy voice;
Take each man's censure, but reserve thy judgment.
Costly thy habit as thy purse can buy,
But not express'd in fancy; rich, not gaudy;
For the apparel oft proclaims the man;
And they in France of the best rank and station

Are most select and generous, chief in that.
Neither a borrower nor a lender be;
For loan oft loses both itself and friend,
And borrowing dulls the edge of husbandry.
This above all: to thine own self be true,
And it must follow, as the night the day,
Thou canst not then be false to any man.

Speech No 2 (relationship with parents)

Do your parents love you? Whether you believe they do or not, I have no intention of trying to persuade you one way or the other. Instead, I'll tell you just when you'll find this out for yourselves. It won't be for some time yet. Actually, not until the grave closes over them or you become parents yourselves. Then you'll know!

I'm not being cynical when I tell you not to worry unduly about this. There's nothing new in it. It's not peculiar to your generation. On the contrary, this has been so as far back as history takes us.

Shakespeare had something to say about it. He wrote,

Crabbed age and youth cannot live together:
Youth is full of pleasance, age is full of care;
Youth like summer morn, age like winter weather;
Youth like summer brave, age like winter bare.

Actually, the relationship between youth and age has improved since Shakespeare's day. We all live together more amicably now.

Mark Twain, the great American author, used to say that when he was fourteen his father was so ignorant he could hardly stand to have him around.

But when he got to be twenty-one he was astonished at how much his father had learned in those seven years.

Today, your parents may seem to you to be people who keep on saying, 'Now, when I was young...' yet never show any sign of having ever been young themselves.

But, believe me, that is how *their* parents seemed to them when *they* were young.

Today, parents are, in my opinion, more tolerant of the behaviour of their sons and daughters than ever before. I wonder, however, whether you are as tolerant of your parents as they had to be of theirs?

I heard recently of a father who was found sitting on the front steps of his home at three in the morning by a policeman.

'What are you doing here?' demanded the policeman.

'Oh,' said the man, 'I've lost my key so I'm waiting for my children to come home and let me in.'

But few parents stay out partying until the early hours of the morning. I wonder how you would react if your parents started doing this and you had to wait up until *they* came in?

Even if you didn't wait up for them, would you not soon be asking such questions as, 'Where have *you* been?' and 'What have *you* been doing?'

Are not these questions precisely those that they now ask you? How would you react to their answers, I wonder?

And how long would it be before you started having doubts?

Would your faith be as strong as theirs?

The other day a woman sent her small son for a couple of pounds of apples. Later, she telephoned the greengrocer to complain that she had weighed the apples and found there was only one pound in the bag.

'I know my scales are correct,' answered the greengrocer. 'Why don't you try weighing your son?'

What we all need – you, the young people of this generation and those of us who are older – is tolerance.

And this even more so when you're part of a one-parent family. When there are two parents, they work off much of their frustration on each other, and you, the juniors in the union, have two adults to work on; sometimes, when too much critical attention is focused on you and your behaviour, you even work one parent against the other. But in a one-parent family you get all the works! Your parent has no one else to turn to or on whom to vent their frustration, and so the spotlight is always on you.

No matter how many the ingredients that make your family, the keynote to its harmony is tolerance. There are, you all know, black and white keys on a piano. Play them together thoughtlessly, without regard to any rules, and you get discord. But, if you understand music and spend some time practising, you can, with the same black and white keys, produce sweet harmonies that move the soul.

If young people and their parents were to spend time studying one another and trying to understand one another, then far more homes would be places of sweet harmony.

Why not try? You start. You'll be surprised at how quickly your people will respond.

17
Old Age

A feature of Holyhead is that it has four old people's clubs and various other organisations for pensioners. Below are speeches actually delivered by the late Gordon Williams, who, as chairman of the local council, had to go around them all at Christmas – and then give speeches at their parties.

'I would have enjoyed all this much more,' he writes, 'had it not been for the fact that I had to make a speech at each of them. The actual delivering of the speeches did not disturb me – they were all appreciative audiences. It was the preparation of the speeches which became a nightmare.'

'You see,' he continues, 'I knew that a small hard core of pensioners would attend the lot, and these would quickly recognise a speech which I had delivered before. Their comments afterwards would, I felt, be – shall we say? – uncomplimentary. There was only one thing to do. Prepare a new speech for each occasion. Believe me, when I came to the seventh, I was really scraping the bottom of the barrel.'

Williams did not inflict all his speeches on his readers, and we shall not be doing so here. But he did leave us with one which has some useful epigrams about Christmas and Christmas presents. It is the first of the three speeches which follow.

Of the other two speeches, one is a straightforward address to old people and the other is one that Williams delivered at a party to celebrate the second anniversary of an old people's club.

Whenever I receive a card from your honorary secretary asking me to attend a Millbank Old People's Club function, those letters 'RSVP' at the bottom remind me of a certain Mr Isaacs whose daughter was getting married.

All the arrangements had been made and Mrs Isaacs was telling her husband about them.

At each expense, he got sadder and sadder. By the time she came to the invitation cards he was really miserable.

'What's this nonsense?' he asked, pointing to the letters RSVP at the bottom of one of the cards.

'Ah,' said his wife, 'that's where your Rebecca has been clever. That means, "Reply Soon Vith Presents".'

This is the time for presents – Christmas presents. May you all receive many.

Someone has said that Christmas presents can be divided into two classes: those you don't like and those you don't get.

Well, I hope you get the sort of presents you like.

Last week I heard a man say that what he liked about Christmas was that you can make people forget the past with a present.

And that's not a bad idea for all of us this Christmas. This is the season when everyone speaks and reads about goodwill. It is the time of times to redress wrongs and repair damaged relationships. Use it.

What did Dickens call it? A kind, forgiving, loving time.

I hope you find it so. I am very grateful to you for asking me to your party, and take this opportunity of wishing you, one and all, a merry Christmas followed by a very happy New Year.

Life has no pleasure nobler than that of friendship. This is a truth which you senior citizens of our town discovered a long time ago. That is why you join one another here so frequently. Seeing you so happy is a pleasant experience and an object lesson to all of us who are honoured to call on you.

People who are getting on in years have found out what is the secret of serenity and happiness. This is something which is denied the young and the middle-aged. Perhaps if we were to come and see you senior citizens more often we should discover what this secret is. Part of it, I am sure, is that happiness is something you cannot chase and catch. Young people spend their life chasing it, but somehow they never quite get hold of it.

I think that I am now old enough to realise that happiness is a gift which comes quietly when one least thinks about it. A good example of this is to be found in a pretty little story called *Golden Windows*. It tells of children playing in the front garden of their home one evening and seeing a palace with windows of gold on a far-off hill. They decide to go to this palace, so they climb their garden wall, walk down their street, through some brambles, across some marshes until finally they reach the hill and climb it.

But at the top, disappointment awaits them. They find that their palace with the golden windows is only an old ruin whose windows have been touched by the setting sun.

They are now very sad so they turn to go home; but there, in the distance, behold! they see their house. From here, though, *that* has golden windows.

Young people strive hard, yet too often lose sight of the things that are really worthwhile.

As we grow old we come to realise what things have real value. One of them is companionship. Surely companionship is the great benefit which comes from these clubs.

Companionship transcends even likes and dislikes. I heard a short time ago a silly story about a man who walked into a café and asked the waitress to bring him grapefruit juice, half water, with seeds in it; scrambled eggs, leathery and water; toast burnt to a frazzle and a pot of lukewarm tea with the leaves floating in it.

The waitress stared at him in amazement for a moment or two, then habit reasserted itself and she asked mechanically, 'Anything else, sir?'

'Yes,' he nodded. 'Just sit opposite me and nag me. You see, I'm homesick.'

Well, the food you get here is much better than that to which the man was accustomed. And no one nags at you here. Here, you may indulge in a little harmless leg-pulling to while away the hours and keep one another interested. Interest, by some means or another, is something you must keep alive because it keeps *you* alive.

May you continue to find your club and companions ever interesting. While you do so this place is a priceless tonic.

Thank you for asking me here. God bless you all.

Speech No 3

I am here tonight to wish your club a happy [second] birthday. Now, I myself have reached that stage in life where I like to have my birthdays remembered but not my age.

But then, of course, I am older than two. I suppose I am what is called middle-aged, which is when you

131

start eating what is good for you and not what you like.

I hope your club has many, many more birthdays. This must be a great day for those who conceived the idea of building these premises. Your baby is two years old today, and a robust, healthy baby it looks to me. Everyone who has had anything whatsoever to do with bringing it to life and rearing it this far must be very proud.

The more I think about these clubs for our senior citizens, the more I like them.

This is a place you can come to when you want peace and quiet. It is a place where you can come to tea every Thursday and chat with people of your own age group.

You can talk about old times – the people you knew in the past, perhaps when you were boys and girls.

I find tracing back families to be a most interesting diversion. I am sure that you have great fun when you indulge in it. If this is not already one of your pastimes I strongly recommend it to you. Try it one afternoon. You will be astonished how quickly that afternoon passes. You will marvel at how characteristics are passed on by fathers and mothers to their children. And, because you are older than I, you will be able to do this in much the same way as the Children of Israel – unto the third and fourth generation.

Indeed, you will realise, not for the first time, I'm sure, how true the Bible is, not only of the Children of Israel but of all people living in a community – of humanity as we know it.

As you think on these things you will discover the truth of that old paradox, 'The boy is the father of the man.' That is to say a pleasant, kind, obliging boy grows up to be a pleasant, kind, obliging man. It is true of the girls, too, of course. The selfish self-centred, gossipy little girl grows up to be a selfish, self-centred gossipy woman, and continues to make things difficult, no matter where she goes. Of course, there are no selfish, self-centred, gossipy little boys! They are all perfect. Indeed, I was surprised to hear one the other day, when asked what a grandmother was, say, 'A grandmother is an old lady who keeps your mother from spanking you.'

Another diversion which you would find interesting is that of tracing how well, or badly, the boys and girls who were clever at school did in the rest of their lives.

You can talk, too, about Holyhead as it was. Some of you will no doubt remember our Harbour of Refuge sheltering hundreds of sailing vessels from tempest.

You can exchange recollections about famous wrecks and rescues; about defunct shipping companies which at one time were very important in the town.

Think back to the days of your youth. Who were the personalities and characters in the town then? Which people amused, interested or annoyed you in those days?

Only last week I was complaining to a friend that there didn't seem to be any characters like those of my youth around today. He cut me short. 'Don't talk nonsense,' he said. 'You and I are the characters today.'

Be that as it may, the past is very important. It is tradition. It is something which ought to be preserved.

It would be an excellent thing for the town if you kept a record of your reminiscences, in writing or on tape. Generations to come would then read or hear them. They would get to know better the place which gave them birth. Yours, and the memories of those who went before you, are our heritage. They are what makes Holyhead individually different from any other town, and to some of us the best town in the world.

May I congratulate you on looking so well, all of you. Being the senior citizens of the town suits you, each one of you. You have a place of honour in our community. Make as much use as you can of your club. Keep on being interested in one another and, indeed, in as many other things as you can.

May God continue to bless you all.

18

Welcoming Foreigners

The first of the speeches that follow was prepared for delivering to a party of Americans visiting Britain. You never know when you may be called upon to address visitors from foreign lands, and it shows the sort of thing you could try to put over on such occasions.

If you are ever asked to address foreign visitors, be as polite and charming as you can. Always remember, they will judge our country by the impression you make on them.

Speech No 1

'The United States of America and Great Britain are two nations separated by a single language.'

I'm sure you've all often heard that quotation. It seems to me to be quite true. For instance, we eat sweets, not candy; we use torches, not flashlights; we travel in lifts, not elevators; our cars have windscreens and boots, while yours have windshields and trunks. American babies wear diapers, but British ones wear nappies. You shine your shoes; we polish ours. What you call garters, we call suspenders; while what *you* call suspenders, we call braces!

Another thing that separates us is, of course, the Atlantic; but with today's magic carpet, which we call Concorde, and those man-made marvels up there circuiting the earth and beaming pictures of events – as they occur – from one side of the ocean to the other, science has diminished it so that its effect today is only slightly more limiting than the English

Channel was decades ago.

It now takes less time to travel by air from London to New York than it does to get from London to Edinburgh by train.

I hope that you are enjoying the look you're taking at us. The more your nation and mine visit each other, the better it is.

I dare say you've noticed we do some things differently from you. For instance, I'm sure you'll say we drive on the wrong side of the road. Er...we call it the *left*-hand side!

No doubt, too, *you've* found some things about *us* that have caused you amusement. The uniforms some of our military men wear: for example, the Beefeaters in the Tower of London, the Chelsea Pensioners in Sir Christopher Wren's magnificent Chelsea Barracks, the breastplated Household Cavalry on Horse Guards Parade and the bearskins of the Guardsmen on sentry duty outside Buckingham Palace.

There is, however, one uniform we both identify the moment we land in our respective countries: the Customs Officer's. He is there watching, no matter what time we arrive. And he can spot-check passengers even after they've passed through the Green Channel, as a friend of mine discovered.

He was already clutching the regulation duty-frees in the usual plastic bag; so started to pray.

'Have you anything else to declare?' demanded the Customs man, eyeing my friend's jumbo-sized suitcase.

'Nothing,' said my friend, 'only clothes – used clothes!' But he had to open it, and the Customs man started to rummage. Suddenly he stopped. His hand had touched something hard; and in a moment he brought it out – a bottle of brandy!

'I thought you said it only contained clothes,' he said menacingly.

'Yes, that's right,' said my friend. 'That's my nightcap.'

The differences between us are, thank heaven, actually of little consequence. They are in no way sinister! All they do is provide our two countries with national character. In essentials we are one.

Our conceptions of freedom, justice, government and democracy are similar.

We like to think that you are like us and that we are like you. Two nations separated by one language, I said earlier. Yes, but welded together by history, war and common experiences. We observe the same moral code, our ideal is peace and goodwill among human beings. So long as we stand side by side at the van of the English-speaking peoples, the torch of freedom will continue to burn.

I don't think anyone can improve on the way a Native American in your army during the last war described the relation between your country and ours. 'You know,' he said, 'when our countries smoked the Pipe of Peace together they sure did inhale.'

And that is why we are glad to see you. The more we learn about one another as individuals and representatives of vocations, professions, trades or occupations, the better we will understand one another. Understanding, you know, begets tolerance, and the more tolerance any one of us can foster in the world, the better it will be for us and our children.

There is no Pipe of Peace here for me to smoke, but there is a drink. It is with affection that I drink to you and your great country. To America!

Bienvenue et soyez le bienvenue, which for others who, like me, are monoglots, means, 'Welcome, and it's nice to have you with us.'

Mademoiselle Smith, une femme professeur, pour notre lycée has very kindly consented to translate what I say into French. I will speak slowly so that she can do this, and everyone will understand. I hope!

Her task, I am told, will be simplified, because, unlike French, so many English words have a number of different meanings. Take, for instance, the English word *fast*. If in French I said I was *vite,* I would be fast; or if I said I was *attaché,* I would still be fast; or if I confessed to being a *dissipateur* – a spendthrift – they would again call me fast; or were I not eating – *ne manger* – that, too, would be fast: *a* fast.

The reports that reach me are that many of you are fast learners, and already converse in English as though you were English people, in accents that have certainly improved from *atroce*.

Congratulations! We are delighted. I am told, too, that great progress is also being made by our own people who speak French, no matter to what degree. These are, of course, the more obvious benefits that the twinning of our towns produces.

But language is not the only thing that has improved from our twinning. It has encouraged a number of our citizens to visit other parts of *la Belle France* and they have had many surprises. One of these tourists was telling me about the time he went to Paris. He had gone to the magnificent Luxembourg Gardens. There he got a considerably greater thrill than at the Folies Bergére, for on a terrace there stood a row of life-size statues of the Queens of France in weathered stone. And one of these bore the name

Mary Stuart. Yes, our own Mary, Queen of Scots. It took him moments to blow away the cobwebs from his memory and remember that she was the widow of the son of your great François the First, who did so much to encourage the arts in your country. For him, during that moment, for the first time in his life, history lived.

Many of you, I'm told, will have to fast when you return to France. Your much-vaunted French cooking has to some extent, this week, lost the Grand Prix. That has, instead, been generously awarded to our bacon, eggs, toast and marmalade. The British breakfast, along with our roast beef and Yorkshire pudding, has won over many discerning stomachs.

And, of course, there is the British pub with its cold refreshing beer. I have heard whispers that some prefer it to today's bistro. No one, though, has said that he prefers beer to wine. Indeed, I understand that you have no difficulty in converting most of your hosts to changing to it. And was that not always so?

Our people have taken you around to see the sights – some of our light industries, and the vessels that ferry people across the Irish Sea to Eire. Industries, schools and commercial institutions you found were as routine here as at home. Our way of life has many basic similarities.

Some of you were taken to see our nearest stately home, Plas Newydd, which is on the other side of the Isle of Anglesey. When you heard the name of the soldier to whose memory the nearby tall column was erected you insisted on climbing to its top to inspect. To those of you who did not go, the statue at the top is that of the first Marquis of Anglesey. You may have heard of him. As Lord Uxbridge he had one of his legs shot off by your forebears. That was at Waterloo.

Yes, it is true to say that we have not always been the great friends and permanent allies that we are today, and for many years fought one another. Be that as it may, no matter. Fighting side by side in two world wars has so cemented our relationship that we have become permanent allies.

Last Sunday, you organised a simple and very touching ceremony at our War Memorial, which pleased the town very much. As your Mayor, wearing his sash of office, laid your wreath at the Memorial, the words of one of our modern writers, Howard Spring, rang in my ears. 'Love', he said, 'for the same thing never makes allies. It's always *hate* for the same thing.'

May we ever hate the same evil. It is in your national character to love freedom, equality and brotherliness and to fight to the death for them. And it is in ours, too.

Ladies and Gentlemen, I ask you to be upstanding and drink a toast to: 'Our Honoured Guests'.

Vive la France!

19
Appeals and Openings

The first of the three speeches that follow is an appeal on behalf of an imaginary organisation concerned with child welfare. The other two are appeals on behalf of the Freedom from Hunger campaign and Help the Aged.

The Freedom from Hunger Campaign speech was delivered from a pulpit, to an audience of about a thousand. The occasion was a concert at which artistes of BBC fame sang solos and duets.

The second and third were delivered in real life by Gordon Williams, who writes, 'When...I began to "preach" on behalf of the Freedom from Hunger Campaign [the audience] were delighted and listened as though spellbound. Perhaps they felt they ought not to laugh too often in church, even though it was a nonconformist church and had none of the religious furnishings of more demonstrative persuasions.' He admits that 'some of the jokes in the speech fell a little flat'. Note that he refers to his brother, a clergyman.

Speech No 1

'It is more blessed to give than to receive' are the words which have caused men to ponder and act generously throughout the Christian era.

Benevolence is a virtue of the highest order. It has brought immeasurable benefits to humanity.

One of the attributes of benevolence is sympathy; indeed, sympathy is the force which triggers off benevolence.

I am sure that your sympathy will be triggered off when I tell you the story of little Ellen Smith.

Until six months ago, her father was abroad with the Navy. Ellen, her mother and three other children lived with her grandmother. Her mother had never wanted Ellen. Her grandmother did, though, and protected her so that she was happy enough. But within the past nine months two calamities occurred in Ellen's life. First, her grandmother died, and second her father was discharged from the Navy and came home to live. He disliked Ellen, and felt her very being an insult to him. She had red hair and he knew of no one in his family who had red hair. Because of this, and the fact that his wife had no time for her, he got to thinking that Ellen was not his child.

Soon he was beating her with a cruel belt. He would keep her locked up alone for days in an attic bedroom in which there were no amenities, not even a light. He made the poor child's life a hell on earth. And in that hell she would still be, if a kindly neighbour had not reported her plight to the society on behalf of which I am appealing this evening.

Ellen Smith now lives at one of its homes. She's become a happy, healthy child, full of life. Slowly, she's forgetting the nightmare days that followed her grandmother's death and her father's homecoming.

I wish you could see her, both now and as she was before she went to the home. If you could, I'm sure she would touch your hearts. But, because it would be wrong of us to make a spectacle of little Ellen Smith, I can't let you see her, even as she is today.

The society that is looking after her needs funds – funds to carry on its excellent work, of which I've given you but one example. I assure you that there are thousands of others.

Will you please give generously? Your support is sorely needed.

Thank you for listening to me so attentively. I hope

I have shown you that this society is worthy of your support and will now ask the stewards to go round and collect your contributions. I assure you that no penny of what you give will be wasted. Thank you very much.

The ending of this speech depends on how you are collecting the money, of course. You will notice that the appeal itself is really the story of Ellen Smith, a victim of child cruelty until she was rescued by the organisation we've invented for the purpose of the speech. This is known as a human-interest story. You will find that it is easily the best way of making such an appeal. People understand a human story much better than the recital of a long list of statistics. What is more, they respond far more generously to the appeal in connection with which it is told.

Speech No 2

Standing here, looking around, I am inclined to wonder whether a mistake has not been made. Have you not got the wrong member of my family here? Surely, this is my reverend brother's forum?

I wonder, too, what I am doing appealing for Hunger Relief with a figure like mine!

For some time before coming here I was at a loss to know why there should be a chairman at all at a concert like this. Eventually, somebody told me.

'You are,' he said, 'like the sprig of parsley that's served with the fish course.'

I don't think he intended that I should interpret this as meaning that I am decorative. And I certainly am not saying that our wonderful artistes look like fish!

But you will, I trust, pardon me the irresistible pun: it's a whale of a concert!

And you are a whale of an audience. Thank you for buying tickets. Thank you for coming. Without you all the effort behind this evening would have been in vain.

And we'd have felt like the mother who said to her little girl, 'I've tried so hard. I've done everything I can to make you good, to make a success of you. But all my efforts have been wasted, and I'm made to look a fool.'

The little girl turned on her mother and said callously, 'Mother, you are a failure!'

Thanks to you, we this evening have not been a failure. Our compère, choir and artistes have all been splendid, too, haven't they?

We're grateful to the gentlemen in the choir, Mrs Gaynor Williams, their accompanist, and Mr Dewi Francis, their conductor. You are always ready to give your splendid services free to any good cause. Listening to you has been a thrilling experience.

The individual artistes and their accompanist deserve our thanks, too. Even those who are not musically minded must surely applaud your very fine performance. Thank you, Mrs Enid Thomas, Mr Richard Rees and Mr Richie Thomas for coming here at a reduced fee, and thank you, Miss Olwen Lewis, for giving your excellent services free.

There are some other good people whom I would like to thank, too: the minister, deacons and members of this church for allowing us the use of it.

Is there anybody else? Oh, yes: the compère and the organisers.

Everybody here tonight is twice blessed. Not only have we had a most enjoyable evening, but we have, too, the satisfaction of knowing that all the money made as a result of this concert will go to one of the most worthy causes on earth today: the Freedom from Hunger Campaign, a charity that has been commended to us by the highest in the land.

Now, there are two forms of charity: one alleviates and the other cures. The first is often prompted by sentiment, the second by Christianity.

The Freedom from Hunger Campaign is, of course, in the second category.

Officials of this organisation see to it that aid is given to the needy in two parts. The first part consists in providing them with sufficient food for a healthy life for the time being. And, believe me, these communities are in dire need. They are not simply underfed or undernourished. Many of their members are literally starving. Too often they are a pitiful prey to hideous diseases from the day they are born, throughout their primitive, insanitary lives, until they reach their inevitably early graves.

And all this is so unnecessary in the world with all the knowledge and resources at its command today.

This is where the second part of the work of the organisation which we are supporting tonight comes in. Officials of the Freedom from Hunger Campaign advise, train and − with funds supplied by good people like you − equip these communities so that in the years ahead they will eventually be self-supporting. Henceforth, they will be kept on the road to prosperity. No longer will they need charity from ourselves or anybody else.

Without our aid their situation is hopeless. And what a shamefully sad thing that is to say, especially when you hear that Freedom from Hunger Campaign field workers say there are really no hopeless situations. No, they are all situations in which people have *grown* hopeless by being in them.

The Freedom from Hunger Campaign brings hope to these. Hope that the future holds for them a better, healthier, more fortunate life. No longer will they be worse off than animals. Their rising generation starts to be more important, more significant. Soon they are like the early Children of Israel, full of hope, planning for the third and fourth generations.

Anyone who helps any human being from degradation, evil superstition or circumstances is surely doing God's work. Anyone who improves the lot of humanity in any part of this old world of ours glorifies God. It is worthy, holy work.

In various ways, you – each one of you – by being here tonight have contributed to this high calling. Thank you.

Speech No 3

'Charity begins at home...but should not end there' is the kind of thinking that prompted Cecil Jackson-Cole to found Help the Aged. Already he was co-founder of Oxfam and was abroad in connection with its work when he had this vision...

In the world there were millions of refugees of all ages. For the young and middle-aged there was hope – possibly rehabilitation; they were able to start a new life. But for the aged – what does the future hold for them? They were too old to start again. There was not time. Many would be gone...within twelve months! So why not do something for them, here and now? What could be done would have to be done at once. An old Latin proverb avers, 'He twice gives who gives quickly.'

And so, in 1961, Cecil Jackson-Cole inaugurated the charity that he called 'Help the Aged Refugees Appeals' to bring positive relief to old people caught up in both man-made and natural disasters.

That is how the national charity for whose support

I am now appealing to you was started.

Today it is called Help the Aged and it gives aid to sick, needy or destitute aged people the whole world over, regardless of race, caste or creed.

In our country it has been foremost in establishing housing for the aged. It is the front line of endowing research by medical science into the needs of the elderly, and, in this field, it feels that a great deal more can be done, and *needs* to be done, to deter the deleterious effects that advancing years so frequently have upon us.

This is not an airy-fairy notion, but the considered opinion of medical men who now, as a result of hefty Help the Aged endowments, research the mysteries of gerontology. This means that, when you support Help the Aged, each of you is supporting a campaign that could be helpful to you yourself. So, tonight, be kind to yourselves, and give generously. Please!

There are many other ways by which Help the Aged improves life for our elderly. It considers day centres to be of prime importance, and supports these in more than one way all over our land. The great bogey of old age is loneliness. At these day centres it is never allowed across the threshold. So important does it consider day centres that Help the Aged often provides a minibus to get aged people to them, even when it itself does not run the day centres.

I could go on and on, but the clock is already ahead of me and I have yet to tell you about some of its work overseas. Why don't you yourselves send a postcard to Help the Aged to ask for more details? Just send to the Help the Aged Head Office in London – get the full address from a telephone directory.

Abroad there is unbelievable poverty, such as we in Britain cannot comprehend. Out there people really are starving. All the problems that we have, they have – but magnified many times.

Take, for instance, housing. In Calcutta they beg for a blanket – that will be their house, their shelter and most prized possession, until they are taken, wrapped up in it, on their final journey to the burning ghat.

In Africa, water is the eternal problem. With grants from Help the Aged, wells are sunk and water, not only for drinking but for irrigation too, brings the aged better lives.

Africa and India have tremendous medical problems. One for which Help the Aged has done a great deal is cataracts. It finances hospitals doing ophthalmic work so that those who were recently blind can now see. For places like Somalia it has even sent out special medical teams to cope with ophthalmic operations.

Welfare work continues in South America. There, Help the Aged initiates and supports self-help schemes such as a laundry in Colombo, a job-creation scheme in Peru and so on.

At Christmas time, the very poor in many places of the Third World bless it for its Christmas meals programme which makes sure that thousands have a special meal and celebration at this time.

When disaster strikes, whether man-made, as in war or insurrection, or as the result of natural causes, such as earthquakes and floods, Help the Aged is in the forefront with material help.

I have tried to give you an all-round picture of the work which Help the Aged does. It is, I know, sketchy, but in the short time at my disposal whatever I say must, of necessity, be inadequate.

Please, though, do as I asked earlier on: write to the Help the Aged Head Office in London for more information. The telephone directory or Directory Enquiries will be able to provide you with the telephone number.

Presently there will be a collection. Please, please, I beg of you, give to it all you dare.

Whatever you give will, I assure you, be gratefully received, and most faithfully applied.

Thank you.

The opening of a garden fête, sale of work or bazaar requires little in the way of a speech. Their organisers want the things opened as quickly as possible, so that the public can circulate and spend their money.

We suggest you say something like this.

The speech

'The customer is always right' was once the motto of many business undertakings. From the kind and cheerful looks on the faces of this afternoon's stallholders, I feel sure that they will treat all their customers with the utmost courtesy and consideration, even should they decide that they are *not* always right!

To me they look really anxious to meet you – all of you. I shouldn't be surprised if some of them were now thinking that I should hurry up so that they can get down to business!

But I, too, have a function in the business side of this afternoon's proceedings. Indeed, from me you get the 'commercial'!

Not only do I recommend everything here and persuade you that you have need of the things on all the stalls, but I am, too, able to assure you that every penny you spend is wanted and will be put to good use.

Your church cannot carry on in the way it does without functions such as this. So please spend as much as you can here. Be extravagant! Spoil yourselves!

Now, there are great numbers of people to thank. There always are in a function such as this. The best way for me to do this is by saying, 'We thank everyone who has helped, or is helping in any way whatsoever, to make this garden fête possible.'

I myself wish it the greatest success.

In the hope that it tops all previous efforts, I have great pleasure in declaring it open.

20
Politics

This book is not concerned with *party* politics, and the making of a proper political speech is beyond its scope. That is a job for the 'expert'. On occasions, however, an inexperienced person is asked to propose or (more briefly) second a vote of thanks to some speaker or speakers at a political meeting. What follows may be helpful. It can be adapted to any political occasion. All you have to do is substitute the name of your party for Party 'B' and another for Party 'A'

Speech No 1

It gives me great pleasure this evening to propose a vote of thanks to our speakers. Listening to them has, I'm sure, been an enlightening experience for all of us.

A short time ago the 'A' Party and ours held public meetings in the same hall within a week of each other.

The son of the caretaker of that hall saw in this an opportunity to sell his four puppies. He put them in a box on which he wrote 'Puppies For Sale' and stood with them at the entrance to the hall. A member of the 'A' Party decided that one of them would be nice for his son.

'Are they "A" puppies?' he asked.

'Oh, yes, sir!' answered the boy.

And so a puppy was sold.

The following week, when our party was holding its meeting, the boy was there again with the remaining puppies.

A member of our party, attracted by them, asked him, 'Are they "B" puppies, son?'

'Yes, sir,' said the boy.

Unfortunately for him, though, the man who had bought a puppy the previous week was standing close by, and heard him.

'Wait a moment,' said this man. 'Last week you told me they were "A" puppies!'

'That's right, sir,' said the boy. 'But *these* aren't – these ones have got their eyes open.'

I'm sure there are many here this evening who have had their eyes opened by what our speakers have said. Indeed, having listened carefully, I confess to seeing more clearly myself.

If the case for our party is presented all over the country in as efficient a manner as we have heard tonight, and people listen properly, then there's no doubt as to the outcome of the next election.

Ladies and gentlemen, I formally move a vote of thanks to our speakers. May they have great good luck and much success always.

Speech No 2

It gives me pleasure to second the vote of thanks proposed by Mr Smith.

Listening to our most able speakers, I couldn't help thinking that it is three bones that will see our campaign through to a successful conclusion: the wishbone, the jawbone and the backbone. The wishbone because it will keep our goal foremost in our minds. The jawbone because it is by talking about our campaign and asking questions about that of others that we will convince people that right is on our side. And the backbone because that will keep us at it until we reach our goal.

The old African witch-doctor can do wonderful things with his bones. We can, too, if every one of us uses the three that I've mentioned for the good of the party.

I now formally second the vote of thanks and I'm sure you would all like to demonstrate your appreciation of the efforts of our speakers in the time-honoured way. [*Applaud.*]

Part 3
Quotations and Jokes

21
Introduction

Part Three concerns itself with the material you will find useful to merge into your chosen speech, whether it is one of your own or taken from the examples in Part Two. In the following sections you will find a host of useful quotations, supported by a comprehensive index, and a number of jokes, some of which you may have heard before, and some you won't. Even those that you *have* heard – and know that *everyone's* heard – can be funny and effective if you play them for their antiquity, their corniness. We've all enjoyed a joke with a groan factor as well as those that produce a belly laugh.

The indexes
You will find a comprehensive index at the back of each section, with the numbers in brackets referring to *the number of the quotation or joke, not to the page*. We have cross-referenced as comprehensively as possible, to help you find what you are looking for quickly and easily. You will also find references in the indexes to concepts as well as to specific types of person or thing, and this device should help you to find just the right support for your speech.

Please note that authors quoted in the quotations are to be found in CAPITALS in the index, whereas if they have merely been referred to in the *text* of a quotation, their names are rendered in upper- and lower-case type.

22
The Quotations

It is more likely that you will want to find an apt or amusing quotation or epigram than to tell a string of jokes. These can be woven into a speech to spice it up or to add relevance to, or support for, what you are saying.

Never be afraid to quote another; you are not plagiarising by so doing, because you will be acknowledging your source. Many witty and apt musings have found voice through the ages touching on countless aspects of life, and people do like to hear an aphorism or otherwise witty saying, often finding that they know the saying but never realised that it was said by so-and-so.

There are, of course, books of quotations, but this collection should excite your interest in digging for the appropriate words to illuminate your speeches. And, of course, quotations always make interesting and amusing reading in their own right.

Accidents
1   Once you start buying first-aid kits you start having accidents. GEORGE MIKES

Achievement, perseverance, success, destiny
2   Everything comes to him who hustles while he waits. THOMAS A EDISON

3   Greatness is not achieved by never falling, but by rising every time we fall. CONFUCIUS

4   To be great is to be misunderstood. R W EMERSON

5   A life of ease is a difficult pursuit. W COWPER

6   The lowest ebb is the turn of the tide. HENRY
WADSWORTH LONGFELLOW

Actors
7   Phoebe Lucas would play a glamorous courtesan with
about as much sex appeal as a haddock! NOËL COWARD

8   They [actors] are a race apart, doomed to go through
life pretending to be somebody else. R F DELDERFIELD

9   Actors like Shakespeare because they can gum on a
lot of crêpe hair, bellow almost anything that comes into
their heads, and then have their Lear taken seriously by
the critics. J B PRIESTLY

10   I remember a landlady who used to split her dining-
room into two halves: straight actors on the left, variety
turns on the right. ERNIE WISE

Adultery
11   *What men call gallantry, and gods adultery*
     Is much more common when the climate's sultry.
     LORD BYRON

12   *A little still she strove, and much repented,*
     And whispering, 'I will ne'er consent' – consented.
     LORD BYRON

13   I love my neighbour as myself, and to avoid coveting
my neighbour's wife I desire to be coveted by her – which
you know is another thing. WILLIAM CONGREVE

14   Hypocrisy...cannot, like adultery or gluttony, be
practised at spare moments. W SOMERSET MAUGHAM

15   *When Pontius wished an edict might be passed*
     That cuckolds should into the sea be cast,

His wife, assenting, thus replied to him:
'But first, my dear, I'd have you learn to swim.'
MATTHEW PRIOR

Advertising
16 We all know nowadays that advertisements can be a fine art; but Nature made that discovery long ago, when birdsong burst into beauty. JULIAN HUXLEY

17 I never read a patent medicine advertisement without being impelled to the conclusion that I am suffering from the particular disease...in its most virulent form.
J K JEROME

18 Advertising is the cheapest way of selling goods, particularly if the goods are worthless. SINCLAIR LEWIS

Advice, Criticism
19 You should never take advice from any man, however well he knows his subject, unless he also knows you. BALAAM

20 Advice is seldom welcome. Those who need it most like it least. SAMUEL JOHNSON
     (A variation on this by LORD CHESTERFIELD is almost the same: 'Advice is seldom welcome; and those who want it the most always like it the least.' Johnson's has the edge, sounding pithier for being a little more terse.)

21 No one wants advice – only corroboration. JOHN STEINBECK

22 I always pass on good advice. It is the only thing to do with it. OSCAR WILDE

23 To consult is to seek another's approval of a course already decided on. AMBROSE BIERCE

24 When a man comes to me for advice I find out the kind of advice he wants, and give it to him. JOSH BILLINGS

25 To ask advice is in nine cases out of ten to tout for flattery. JOHN CHURTON COLLINS

26 I have lived some thirty years on this planet, and I have yet to hear the first syllable of valuable or even earnest advice from my seniors. H D THOREAU

27 Criticism takes the cumbersome mess of creative work and distils it into a fine essence. OSCAR WILDE

28 One cannot attack a bad book without showing off. W H AUDEN

29 Friendly attacks should begin with faint praise, but be careful not to use adjectives or phrases of which the publisher can make use in advertisements. JOHN BETJEMAN

30 The critic is often an unsuccessful author, almost always an inferior one. LEIGH HUNT

31 This is not a novel to be tossed aside lightly. It should be thrown with great force. DOROTHY PARKER

Age/ageing/youth
32 The old believe everything; the middle-aged suspect everything; the young know everything. OSCAR WILDE

33 *Lately I appear*
To have reached that stage
When people look old
Who are only my age. RICHARD ARMOUR

34 What find you better or more honourable than age? Take the pre-eminence of it in everything: in old friends, in old wine, in an old pedigree. SHAKERLEY MARMION

35 Old age is always fifteen years older than I am. BERNARD M BARUCH

36 *The gardener's rule applies to youth and age:*
When young 'sow wild oats', but when old
   grow sage. H J BYRON

37 I've never known a person to live to 110 or more, and
then die, to be remarkable for anything else. JOSH BILLINGS

38 When a man falls into his anecdotage it is a sign for
him to retire. BENJAMIN DISRAELI

39 You know you're getting old when the candles cost
more than the cake. BOB HOPE

40 The inevitable result of any attempt to prolong youth
is a graceless old age. CLIVE JAMES

41 Passing your eightieth birthday is no great achievement. You just sit still and it happens. ANGUS MCBEAN

42 Anyone can get old. All you have to do is live long
enough. GROUCHO MARX

43 When you've reached a certain age and think that a
facelift or a trendy way of dressing will make you feel
twenty years younger, remember – nothing can fool a
flight of stairs. DENIS NORDEN

44 Forty is the old age of youth, fifty is the youth of old
age. VICTOR HUGO

45 It's no use growing older if you only learn new ways
of misbehaving yourself. SAKI

46 When your friends begin to flatter you on how young
you look, it's a sure sign you're getting old. MARK TWAIN

Ancestors
47 To have an ancestor who was hanged for sheep-
stealing gives me a certain social standing. ROBERT MORLEY

Anger

48 Peace of mind is better than giving them a piece of your mind. J P MCEVOY

49 Never forget what a man says to you when he's angry. HENRY WARD BEECHER

50 Anger is not only inevitable, it is also necessary. Its absence means indifference, the most disastrous of human failings. ARTHUR PONSONBY

Animals/birds

51 The sloth lives his life upside down. He is perfectly comfortable that way. If the blood rushes to his head, nothing happens because there is nothing to work on.
WILL CUPPY

52 Animals generally return the love you lavish on them by a swift bite in passing – not unlike friends and wives.
GERALD DURRELL

53 All I know of birds to this date is that sparrows are the ones that are not pigeons. ALAN COREN

54 The Love Bird is one hundred per cent faithful to his mate – who is locked into the same cage. WILL CUPPY

55 There is nothing in which the birds differ more from man than the way in which they can build and yet leave a landscape as it was before. ROBERT LYND

56 Many birds and beasts are...as fit to go to Heaven as many human beings – people who talk of their seats there with as much confidence as if they had booked them at a box-office. LEIGH HUNT

57 Man is the only animal that blushes – or needs to.
MARK TWAIN

Antagonism/Adversity

58   Always forgive your enemies; nothing annoys them so much. OSCAR WILDE

59   There is no arguing with Johnson, for when his pistol misses fire he knocks you down with the butt end of it. OLIVER GOLDSMITH

60   I dislike arguments of any kind. They are always vulgar, and often convincing. OSCAR WILDE

Apology

61   Apologise: to lay the foundations for a future offence. AMBROSE BIERCE

62   It's a good rule in life never to apologise. The right sort of people don't want apologies, and the wrong sort take a mean advantage of them. P G WODEHOUSE

Argument/bigotry

63   A bigot is one who is obstinately and zealously attached to an opinion that you do not entertain. AMBROSE BIERCE

64   *A man convinced against his will*
     Is of the same opinion still. SAMUEL BUTLER

Aristocracy

65   Honour is a luxury for aristocrats, but it is a necessity for hall-porters. G K CHESTERTON

66   Titles distinguish the mediocre, embarrass the superior and are disgraced by the inferior. GEORGE BERNARD SHAW

Art/architecture

67   Any fool can paint a picture but it takes a wise man to be able to sell it. SAMUEL BUTLER

68   Architecture approaches nearer than any other art to being irrevocable, because it is so difficult to get rid of.
G K CHESTERTON

69   All architecture is great architecture after sunset.
G K CHESTERTON

70   A courageous and partly successful attempt to disguise a gasworks as a racquets court. PETER FLEMING (on the Shakespeare Memorial Theatre, Stratford-on-Avon).

71   If you went round the National Portrait Gallery without knowing who the portraits were of, you would be as bored as if they were so much wallpaper. LORD DAVID CECIL

72   I must have gone on looking at pictures for ten years before I would honestly admit to myself that they merely bored me. ALDOUS HUXLEY

73   Art, like nature, makes its own laws as it goes along.
LAMBERT JEFFRIES

74   The business of art is to colour the mind; the business of science is to straighten it. LAMBERT JEFFRIES

75   'What are you painting?' I said. 'Is it the Heavenly Child?'
        'No,' he said, 'it is a cow.' STEPHEN LEACOCK

76   Art is a lie which makes us realise the truth.
PABLO PICASSO

Babies
77   We have never understood the fear of some parents about babies getting mixed up in a hospital. What difference does it make as long as you get a good one?
HEYWOOD BROUN

78   More twins are being born these days. Maybe it's because kids haven't the courage to come into the world alone. STAN BURNS

79   Give an average baby a fair chance, and if it doesn't do something it oughtn't to a doctor should be called in at once. J K JEROME

Ballet
80   I can think of nothing more kinky than a prince chasing a swan around all night. ROBERT HELPMAN

81   If dancing is the expression of lovemaking it is the oddest in the world, for the lady is (often) forgotten. The gentleman capers by himself, and he expresses his passion by seeing how many jumps he can take, how often he can quiver his feet before he comes down, and how eminently he can stand on one leg. LEIGH HUNT

Banks
82   *Most banks will gladly grant a loan,*
   In fact they often speed it;
   The only thing that they require
   Is proof that you don't need it. F G KERNAN

83   Banks don't make pleasant shareholders. JULIAN SHUCKBURGH (publisher)

Beards
84   Charlemagne was renowned for the length of his beard. It was said that he could kneel on it, though it is not recorded why this was necessary. NICHOLAS BENTLEY

85   The best after-shave is cold water, but clever industrial chemists have persuaded many men to put all kinds of muck on their faces. LAMBERT JEFFRIES

Beauty
86   All heiresses are beautiful. JOHN DRYDEN

87   Beauty, when most uncloth'd, is clothèd best.
PHINEAS FLETCHER

88   *In beauty faults conspicuous grow:*
The smallest speck is seen on snow. JOHN GAY

89   I'm tired of all this nonsense about beauty being only skin-deep... What do you want? An adorable pancreas?
JEAN KERR

Bed
90   There is not a single proverb in favour of early rising that appeals to the higher nature of man. ROBERT LYND

91   No human being believes that any other human being has a right to be in bed when he himself is up. ROBERT LYND

Behaviour
92   Selfishness is not living as one wishes to live: it is asking others to live as one wishes to live. And unselfishness is letting other people's lives alone, not interfering with them. Selfishness always aims at creating around it an absolute uniformity of type. Unselfishness recognises infinite variety of type as a delightful thing, acquiesces in it, enjoys it. OSCAR WILDE

93   When men speak ill of thee, so live that no one will believe them. PLATO

94   The measure of a man's real character is what he would do if he knew he would never be found out.
THOMAS B MACAULAY

Books
95   Many modern novels have a beginning, a muddle and an end. PHILIP LARKIN

96   If you believe everything you read, better not read.
GEORGE JOHNSTONE

Boredom

97　A bore is a person who talks when you wish him to listen. AMBROSE BIERCE

98　The capacity for human beings to bore one another seems to be vastly greater than that of any other animals. H L MENCKEN

Business/work

99　I like work; it fascinates me. I can sit and look at it for hours. I love to keep it by me; the idea of getting rid of it nearly breaks my heart. J K JEROME

100　A dinner lubricates business. LORD STOWELL

101　The reasonable man adapts himself to the world; the unreasonable one persists in trying to adapt the world to himself. Therefore all progress depends on the unreasonable man. GEORGE BERNARD SHAW

Cars

102　A conservation area is a place where you can't build a garage but you can build a motorway.
JAMES GLADSTONE

Charity

103　It is not enough to help the feeble up, but to support him after. WILLIAM SHAKESPEARE

104　The living need charity more than the dead.
GEORGE ARNOLD

Children

105　There are two classes of travel: first-class and with children. ROBERT BENCHLEY

106　People who say they sleep like a baby usually don't have one. LEO J BURKE

107 How many children have acquired a bad habit as a result of having it attributed to them! MICHAEL BURN

108 Anybody who hates children and dogs can't be all bad. W C FIELDS

109 The main purpose of children's parties is to remind you that there are children more awful than your own. KATHERINE WHITEHORN

Christmas
110 Christmas: a day set apart and consecrated to gluttony, drunkenness, maudlin sentiment, gift-taking, and public dullness. AMBROSE BIERCE

111 When I'm King there will be a law that no shop will be allowed to sell anything Christmassy until December 1st. PAUL DANIELS

112 I have a carefully worked-out plan for doing the Christmas shopping. It's called panic. PAUL DANIELS'

113 I am more and more convinced that Scrooge was one of the most sensible men I have ever read about. MICHAEL GREEN

Cinema
114 A sixpenny seat meant that you occupied a hard bench almost within touching distance of the brass rail enclosing the orchestra pit, and here the screen was enormous. Gloria Swanson's eyes looked like Siberian lakes. R F DELDERFIELD

115 I want a movie that starts with an earthquake and works up to a climax. SAM GOLDWYN (attributed)

116 The length of a film should be directly related to the endurance of the human bladder. ALFRED HITCHCOCK

Clothes

117 A little boy and a little girl were looking at a picture of Adam and Eve. 'Which is which?' one asked. 'I don't know,' said the other, 'but I could tell if they had their clothes on.' SAMUEL BUTLER

118 The kilt is an unrivalled garment for fornication and diarrhoea. JOHN MASTERS

119 All dress is fancy dress, isn't it, except our natural skins. GEORGE BERNARD SHAW

120 *Spent six consecutive weeks without stopping,*
In one continuous round of shopping...
Yet when we last met there was utter despair
Because she had nothing whatever to wear!
WILLIAM ALLEN BUTLER

121 When a woman wears a low-cut gown, what does she expect you to do: look or not look? WILLIAM FEATHER

Collecting

122 When a thing is old, broken and useless we throw it on the dust-heap, but when it is sufficiently old, sufficiently broken and sufficiently useless we give money for it. SAMUEL BUTLER

Cooking

123 Heaven sends good meat but the Devil sends cooks.
DAVID GARRICK

124 She was a good cook, as cooks go; and, as cooks go, she went. SAKI

Countryside

125 The countryside is laid out in a haphazard, sloppy fashion, offensive to the tidy mind. ALAN BRIEN

126 A pleasant excursion to collect wild flowers... We collected a daisy and fifty-nine things that weren't.
ALAN COREN

Cricket
127 Of all games and sports, cricket appears to be most trying to the temper, for a player cannot lose his wicket without being put out. THOMAS HOOD

128 My own speciality...was to use the bat the wrong way round and present the triangular side to the ball. The results pass all expectation, the ball flying off quite unpredictably. ARTHUR MARSHALL

129 Cricket is the only game where the major part of the team can just idle around and watch a few of their number do the work. GEORGE MIKES

130 Here is a game so doggedly peculiar and dangerous that no foreign nations...have ever adopted it. PETER USTINOV

Crime/justice
131 In the army, 'crime' may range from being unshaven on parade...to irrevocably perforating your rival in love with a bayonet. IAN HAY

132 In the course of justice none of us should see salvation. WILLIAM SHAKESPEARE

133 Justice is always violent to the offending, for every man is innocent in his own eyes. DANIEL DEFOE

Cynicism
134 A cynic is a blackguard whose faulty vision sees things as they are, not as they ought to be. AMBROSE BIERCE

135 The worst government is the most moral. One composed of cynics is often very tolerant and humane.
H L MENCKEN

136 The power of accurate observation is often called cynicism by those who have not got it. GEORGE BERNARD SHAW

Death
137 It's not that I'm afraid to die. I just don't want to be there when it happens. WOODY ALLEN

138 *Swans sing before they die – 'twere no bad thing*
Should certain persons die before they sing.
S T COLERIDGE

139 Self-decapitation is an extremely difficult, not to say dangerous, thing to attempt. W S GILBERT

140 If all dead people had tombs like that of King Cheops, the living would barely have standing room on the earth. LAMBERT JEFFRIES

141 Waldo is one of those people who would be enormously improved by death. SAKI

Dentists
142 A dentist is a prestidigitator who puts metal in your mouth and pulls coins out of your pocket. AMBROSE BIERCE

143 I detest everything about the twentieth century except its dentistry. A L ROWSE

Dignity
144 The surest way of losing one's dignity is to stand on it. LAMBERT JEFFRIES

Doctors
145 God heals, the doctor takes the fee. BENJAMIN FRANKLIN

146 *Physicians of the Utmost Fame*
Were called at once; but when they came

They answered, as they took their Fees,
'There is no Cure for this Disease'. HILAIRE BELLOC

147 People often say to me, 'Vets must know just as much as doctors,' but when it comes to the crunch they are never very keen to let me treat them. JAMES HERRIOT

148 He wrote a doctor's hand – the hand which from the beginning of time has been so disastrous to the pharmacist and so profitable to the undertaker. MARK TWAIN

Dreams
149 Dreams are, of course, tremendously significant, and, *if dreamt properly,* and subsequently analysed properly, should at once reveal your normal hatred of your mother.
W C SELLAR and R J YEATMAN

Drink
150 Abstainer: a weak person who yields to the temptation of denying himself a pleasure. AMBROSE BIERCE

151 Drink because you are happy, never because you are miserable. G K CHESTERTON

152 No animal ever invented anything as bad as drunkenness – or as good as drink. G K CHESTERTON

153 I never drink anything stronger than gin before breakfast. W C FIELDS

154 The Swiss love to pour a little cognac into everything... At a dinner I attended in Lausanne an Englishman tasted so much brandy in the soup that he lifted his plate of consommé and declared solemnly, 'Ladies and gentlemen – the King!' GEORGE MIKES

155 Water, taken in moderation, cannot hurt anybody.
MARK TWAIN

Education

156 Education does not mean teaching people to know what they do not know: it means teaching them to behave as they do not behave. JOHN RUSKIN

157 Colleges hate geniuses just as convents hate saints.
R W EMERSON

158 Education has for its objects the formation of character. HERBERT SPENCER

159 I am wholly against children wasting their time in the idleness of what is called education. WILLIAM COBBETT

160 Examinations are formidable even to the best prepared, for the greatest fool may ask more than the wisest can answer. C C COLTON

161 Nothing that is worth knowing can be taught. OSCAR WILDE

Egotism

162 *I* is the most popular letter in the alphabet. OLIVER HERFORD

163 To love oneself is the beginning of a lifelong romance. OSCAR WILDE

English

164 An Englishman, even when he is alone, forms an orderly queue of one. GEORGE MIKES

165 Many may wonder how the English acquired their reputation of not working as hard as most Continentals. I am able to solve the mystery. They acquired this reputation by not working as hard. GEORGE MIKES

Epitaphs

166 *Here lies my wife: so let her lie!*
   Now she's at rest, and so am I! JOHN DRYDEN

167 *Life is a jest, and all things show it.*
   I thought so once; but now I know it.
   JOHN GAY (for his own tombstone)

168 *Beneath this slab*
   John Brown is stowed.
   He watched the ads
   And not the road. OGDEN NASH

169 *I'm Smith of Stoke, aged sixty-odd;*
   I've lived without a dame
   From youth-time on; and would to God
   My dad had done the same
   THOMAS HARDY (on a pessimist)

170 *This is the grave of Mike O'Day*
   Who died maintaining his right of way.
   His right was clear, his will was strong,
   But he's just as dead as if he'd been wrong. ANON

Etiquette
171 Curtsey while you're thinking what to say. It saves
time. LEWIS CARROL

172 They say courtesy costs nothing, but it's surprising
how many people can't seem to afford it. J BASIL BOOTHROYD

Experience
173 Experience teaches slowly. J A FROUDE

174 *For sterile wearience and drearience*
   Depend, my boy, upon experience. OGDEN NASH

Exploration
175 Choose your companions carefully; you may have to
eat them. W C SELLAR and R J YEATMAN

Face
176 The eyes are the silent orators of the mind. Like all

orators, they are apt to deceive. LAMBERT JEFFRIES

177 Be true to your teeth lest your teeth be false to you.
DEREK ROY

178 A face like a carving abandoned as altogether too
unpromising for completion. H G WELLS

Failure
179 Nothing succeeds, they say, like success. And
certainly nothing fails like failure. MARGARET DRABBLE

Family
180 Home is the girl's prison and the woman's
workhouse. GEORGE BERNARD SHAW

181 He that hath wife and children hath given hostages to
fortune; for they are impediments to great enterprises
either of virtue or mischief. FRANCIS BACON

Food
182 Cauliflower is nothing but cabbage with a college
education. MARK TWAIN

183 A fork is an instrument used chiefly for the purpose
of putting dead animals into the mouth. AMBROSE BIERCE

184 The waiter should bring in a small dish of olives
exactly as if he were carrying John the Baptist's head on a
charger. PAUL EDWARDS

185 The food regulations...allow the meat industry to use
all sorts of ingredients – many of which would once have
been sent to the knacker's yard as rubbish – and get away
with calling them meat. MIKE FOXWELL (on hamburgers
and sausages)

186 He who does not mind his belly will hardly mind
anything else. SAMUEL JOHNSON

187 If you are ever at a loss to support a flagging conversation, introduce the subject of eating. LEIGH HUNT

188 Things that are said to do one good generally taste of sawdust and burnt rubber. R W B HOWARTH

189 There was only one occasion in my life when I put myself on a strict diet...and it was the most miserable afternoon I've ever spent. DENIS NORDEN

Fortune-tellers
190 How happy are astrologers, who are believed if they tell one truth to a hundred lies, while other people lose all credit if they tell one lie to a hundred truths. FRANCESCO GUICCIARDINI (16th century)

191 If the Delphic priestess was visited by a king or general about to do battle, she was likely to say that a great army was destined to suffer defeat; and, unless both sides ran away, it usually did. E V KNOX

Freedom
192 Freedom is the right to tell people what they do not want to hear. GEORGE ORWELL

193 It was only after our great war for freedom [1914-18], and to make the world safe for democracy, that we were all clamped into the passport system. J B PRIESTLY

194 Englishmen will never be slaves: they are free to do whatever the government and public opinion allow them to do. GEORGE BERNARD SHAW

Friends
195 Great men taken up in any way are profitable friends. THOMAS CARLYLE

196 The only reward of virtue is virtue; the only way to have a friend is to be one. R WALDO EMERSON

197 True friendship is like sound health: the value of it is seldom known until it is lost. C C COLTON

198 While your friend holds you affectionately by both your hands, you are safe, for you can watch both of his. AMBROSE BIERCE

199 *Of all the plagues, good Heaven, thy wrath can send,*
Save me, oh save me, from the candid friend.
GEORGE CANNING

200 Money can't buy friends, but you can get a better class of enemy. SPIKE MILLIGAN

201 Animals are such agreeable friends – they ask no questions, they pass no criticisms. GEORGE ELIOT

202 Anyone can sympathise with the sufferings of a friend, but it requires a fine nature to sympathise with a friend's success. OSCAR WILDE

Funerals
203 As grand and griefless as a rich man's funeral.
SYDNEY DOBELL

Future
204 This is the first age that has paid much attention to the future, which is rather ironic since we may not have one. ARTHUR C CLARKE

205 The future is something which everyone reaches at the rate of sixty minutes an hour. C S LEWIS

206 The best thing about the future is that it comes only one day at a time. ABRAHAM LINCOLN

Gambling
207 The urge to gamble is so universal and its practice so pleasurable that I assume it must be evil. HEYWOOD BROUN

208 *If you can make a heap of all your winnings*
And risk it on one turn of pitch-and-toss...
You'll be an ass, my son. LAMBERT JEFFRIES

209 The race is not always to the swift, nor the battle to the strong – but that's the way we bet. DAMON RUNYON

Gardening
210 I value my garden more for being full of blackbirds than of cherries. JOSEPH ADDISON

211 A weed is a plant whose virtues have not yet been discovered. RALPH WALDO EMERSON

212 One of the most pleasing sounds of springtime, to be heard all over the country, is the contented cooing of osteopaths as Man picks up his garden spade.
OLIVER PRITCHETT

Genius
213 I have nothing to declare except my genius.
OSCAR WILDE

214 Genius is the capacity for evading hard work.
ELBERT HUBBARD

Hair
215 Philip of Macedon made a man a judge. Finding later that the man's hair and beard were dyed, he removed him, saying, 'I cannot think that a man who is faithless in his hair can be trusty in his deeds.' PLUTARCH

Happiness
216 A lifetime of happiness! No man could bear it; it would be hell on earth. GEORGE BERNARD SHAW

217 We have no more right to consume happiness without producing it than to consume wealth without producing it.
GEORGE BERNARD SHAW

History

218 History is an account, mostly false, of events, mostly unimportant, which are brought about by rulers, mostly knaves, and soldiers, mostly fools. AMBROSE BIERCE

219 People flock to Stonehenge on fine weekends, pay their money, take a good, long, meaningless look, and drive off leaving a lot of orange peel and Coke cans, after the manner of culture-seekers the world over. J BASIL BOOTHROYD

Holidays

220 The drawback of all seaside places is that half the landscape is unavailable...being covered with useless water. NORMAN DOUGLAS

221 No holiday is ever anything but a disappointment. ALDOUS HUXLEY

Honesty

222 It's discouraging to think how many people are shocked by honesty and how few by deceit. NOËL COWARD

223 If one tells the truth, one is sure, sooner or later, to be found out. OSCAR WILDE

224 What people call insincerity is simply a method by which we can multiply our personalities. OSCAR WILDE

225 Always be sincere, whether you mean it or not. MICHAEL FLANDERS

226 We must make the world honest before we can honestly say to our children that honesty is the best policy. GEORGE BERNARD SHAW

Horses

227 A horse is dangerous at both ends and uncomfortable in the middle. IAN FLEMING

228 He flung himself on his horse and rode off madly in all directions. STEPHEN LEACOCK

Hospitality
229 Hospitality is the virtue which induces us to feed and lodge certain persons who are not in need of food and lodging. AMBROSE BIERCE

Hotels
230 [To make tea in the bedroom] you have...to mix together a plastic envelope containing too much sugar, a small plastic pot of something which is not milk but has curdled anyway, and a thin brown packet seemingly containing the ashes of a cremated mole. FRANK MUIR

Humanity
231 Conscience is thoroughly well bred and soon leaves off talking to those who don't wish to hear it.
SAMUEL BUTLER

232 The end of the human race will be that it will eventually die of civilisation. RALPH WALDO EMERSON

233 Knowledge without integrity is dangerous and dreadful. SAMUEL JOHNSON

234 There is no more mean, stupid, dastardly, pitiful, selfish, spiteful, envious, ungrateful animal than the public. It is the greatest of cowards, for it is afraid of itself.
WILLIAM HAZLITT

235 The world is a comedy to those that think, a tragedy to those that feel. HORACE WALPOLE

Housework
236 The trouble about housework is that whatever you do seems to lead to another job to do or a mess to clear up.
MONICA DICKENS

237 A clothes line will only snap if the ground beneath it is muddy. FAITH HINES and PAM BROWN

Humour
238 The marvellous thing about a joke with a double meaning is that it can mean only one thing. RONNIE BARKER

239 Everything is funny as long as it happens to someone else. WILL ROGERS

240 Humour is like a frog. If you dissect it, it dies.
MARK TWAIN

Hunting
241 One knows so well the popular idea of health. The English country gentleman galloping after a fox. The unspeakable in full pursuit of the uneatable. OSCAR WILDE

242 While a street-boy who threw a kitten to a crowd of dogs would be rightly condemned, his counterpart who co-operates in urging on a pack of hounds to tear a stag or a fox to pieces is acclaimed as a promising sportsman.
PATRICK MOORE

243 When a man wants to murder a tiger he calls it sport; but when the tiger wants to murder him he calls it ferocity.
GEORGE BERNARD SHAW

Husbands and wives
244 Being pregnant is a very boring six months... It's an occupational hazard of being a wife. PRINCESS ANNE

245 A wife is to thank God her husband has faults... A husband without faults is a dangerous observer. MARQUIS OF HALIFAX

246 In marriage a man becomes slack and selfish, and undergoes a fatty degeneration of his moral being. ROBERT LOUIS STEVENSON

Ignorance

247 Ignoramus: a person unacquainted with certain kinds of knowledge familiar to yourself, and having certain other kinds that you know nothing about. AMBROSE BIERCE

248 Everybody is ignorant, only on different subjects. WILL ROGERS

Illness

249 There are those who divide their lives into two parts: 'Before my operation' and 'Since my operation'. RADIO DOCTOR

250 Never talk about your health. When people say, 'How are you?' they don't really want to know. NOEL STREATFIELD

Imagination

251 The Right Honourable gentlemen is indebted to his memory for his jests, and to his imagination for his facts. R B SHERIDAN (of Henry Dundas, MP)

252 To treat your facts with imagination is one thing; to imagine your facts is another. JOHN BURROUGHS

Insults

253 A modest little man, with much to be modest about. WINSTON CHURCHILL (of Clement Attlee, attributed)

254 He could not see a belt without hitting below it. MARGOT ASQUITH (of Lloyd George)

255 If I never see that woman again, it's too soon. GROUCHO MARX

256 She ran the gamut of emotions, from A to B. DOROTHY PARKER (of Katharine Hepburn)

257 Someone cruelly pointed out in print that I looked like an unmade bed. DYLAN THOMAS

258 He is an old bore; even the grave yawns for him.
H BEERBOHM TREE

Irish
259 Take the Blarney Stone. Only the Irish could persuade people to kiss a stone the Norman soldiers had urinated on. DAVE ALLEN

260 The Irish don't know what they want and are prepared to fight to the death to get it. SIDNEY LITTLEWOOD

Journalism
261 The hardest-worked word in my vocabulary was 'alleged'. It can steer you through a mile of rapids.
R F DELDERFIELD

262 Donald Cameron had no qualifications for any profession...so he resolved to try his fortune as a journalist. A G MACDONELL

263 A mixture of arrogance, pomposity and naïveté is shown by supposedly intelligent men and women who think they have a divine right to go on producing the sort of paper *they* like, irrespective of whether enough people want to read it. ANGUS MAUDE

264 *You cannot hope to bribe or twist*
Thank God! the British journalist.
But, seeing what the man will do
Unbribed, there's no occasion to. HUMBERT WOLFE

Law
265 To appeal, in law, is to put the dice back in the box for another throw. AMBROSE BIERCE

266 On the whole barristers are more interested in *their* briefs than in a girl's. JILLY COOPER

267 The Common Law of England has been laboriously

built up about a mythical figure – the figure of 'the reasonable man'. A P HERBERT

Letters
268 At any given moment in the last few years there have been ten letters which I absolutely *must* write, thirty which I *ought* to write and fifty which any other person in my position *would* have written. Probably I have written two.
A A MILNE

Life
269 Life was always like this. Just as something nice and interesting occurred, destiny must intervene with some pressing engagement. CONRAD AIKEN

270 Life is a joke that's just begun. W S GILBERT

271 He had decided to live for ever or die in the attempt.
JOSEPH HELLER

272 Truly, there is a tide in the affairs of men; but there is no gulf stream flowing forever in one direction. J R LOWELL

London
273 This is Soho, where anything goes, and just make sure it is not your wallet. LEN DEIGHTON

274 The Gulf Stream, as it nears the shores of the British Isles...rises into the air, turns into soup and comes down in London. STEPHEN LEACOCK

275 One cannot frequent London restaurants and be utterly ignorant of Italian. E V LUCAS

Love
276 The test of true love is whether you can endure the thought of cutting your sweetheart's toenails.
W N P BARBELLION

277 Platonic love is love from the neck up. THYRA S WINSLOW

278 Love ceases to be a pleasure when it ceases to be a secret. APHRA BEHN (1640-89)

279 A lover without indiscretion is no lover at all. THOMAS HARDY

280 In the Soviet Union there is no mystical or obscure treatment of love, such as decadent Western poets use. We sing of how a young man falls in love with a girl because of her industrial output. STEPHAN PETROVIV

Lying
281 If society needed any further proof that the earl was there, the servant persistently asserted that he was not at home. G K CHESTERTON

282 She's too crafty a woman to invent a new lie when an old one will do. W SOMERSET MAUGHAM

283 If you can't invent a really convincing lie, it's often better to stick to the truth. ANGELA THIRKELL

Madness
284 It is more comfortable to be mad and not know it than to be sane and have one's doubts. G B BURGIN

285 Great wits are sure to madness near allied. JOHN DRYDEN

Marriage
286 I asked Maureen when she was going to get married, but she says why buy a book when you can join a circulating library. MICHAEL GREEN

287 All marriages are happy. It's the living together afterwards that causes all the trouble. RAYMOND HULL

288 Many a man in love with a dimple makes the mistake

of marrying the whole girl. STEPHEN LEACOCK

289 Marriage is at best a dangerous experiment.
T L PEACOCK

290 When a girl marries she exchanges the attentions of
many men for the inattention of one. HELEN ROWLAND

291 What a fuss there would be if people had to pay the
minister as much to marry them as they have to pay a
lawyer to get them a divorce. CLAIRE TREVOR

292 'I don't believe,' said Mr Prendergast, 'that people
would ever fall in love or want to be married if they hadn't
been told about it. It's like abroad: no one would want to
go there if they hadn't been told it existed.' EVELYN WAUGH

Meekness
293 It's going to be fun to see how long the meek can
keep the earth when they inherit it. KIN HUBBARD

Memory
294 It's a poor sort of memory that only works
backwards. LEWIS CARROL

295 A man's memory is what he forgets with. O SHEPARD

Money
296 *That money talks*
I'll not deny.
I heard it once –
It said Goodbye. RICHARD ARMOUR

297 To be clever enough to get all that money, one must
be stupid enough to want it. G K CHESTERTON

298 Money nowadays seems to be produced with a
natural homing instinct for the Treasury. DUKE OF
EDINBURGH

299 Poverty is no disgrace to a man, but it is confoundedly inconvenient. SYDNEY SMITH

300 I've been poor and I've been rich – rich is better. SOPHIE TUCKER

301 Let us all live within our means, even if we have to borrow money to do it. ARTEMUS WARD

Motoring
302 Second-hand car dealers, like cats, can sense when someone is afraid of them. DENIS NORDEN

Murder
303 Every murderer is probably somebody's old friend. AGATHA CHRISTIE

304 If once a man indulges himself in murder, very soon he comes to think very little of robbing, and from robbing he comes next to drinking and Sabbath-breaking, and from that to incivility and procrastination. Once begin upon this downward path, you never know where you are to stop. THOMAS DE QUINCEY

Music
305 One ought to pack one's ears with cotton wool at a concert where Sir Henry Wood conducts. Otherwise the music is apt to distract one's attention. W N P BARBELLION

306 Brass bands are all very well in their place – outside and several miles away. THOMAS BEECHAM

307 I'm a flute-player, not a flautist. I don't have a flaut and I've never flauted. JAMES GALWAY

308 The traditional exhibitionism on the first and last nights of the Prom season...has nothing to do with the music but everything to do with the accident that it is all being televised. SPIKE HUGHES

309 Tenors are noble, pure and heroic, and get the soprano. But baritones are born villains. LEONARD WARREN

Names
310 Suppose our word for rose had come from the Netherlands...anglicised as 'stinkbloom'. What follows? 'My love is like a red, red stinkbloom'? ARTHUR MARSHALL

311 Groucho is not my real name. I'm breaking it in for a friend. GROUCHO MARX

312 The common Welsh name Bzjxxllwcp is pronounced Jackson. MARK TWAIN

Opinion
313 When I want your opinion I'll give it to you. LAURENCE PETER

314 Refusing to have an opinion is a way of having one. LUIGI PIRANDELLO

315 When people agree with me I always feel I must be wrong. OSCAR WILDE

Parents
316 Parents are the last people on earth who ought to have children. SAMUEL BUTLER

317 Have you a young daughter about fifteen? Have a heart-to-heart talk with her on the facts of life. Believe me, you'll learn plenty. VIC OLIVER

318 The thing that impresses me most about America is the way parents obey their children. DUKE OF WINDSOR

Parties
319 A drinks party...normally consists of a room packed full of people, all rapidly talking to each other while eagerly looking for someone else. CINDY BLAKE

320 I don't know how you feel about going to parties in fancy dress, but as a source of pleasure I have always ranked it somewhere on a level with cleaning the oven.
DENIS NORDEN

People
321 Lovers of Humanity generally hate people and children. ROY CAMPBELL

322 Every man has one thing he can do better than anyone else, and usually it is reading his own handwriting.
NORMAN COLLIE

Pessimism
323 The optimist proclaims that we live in the best of all possible worlds; the pessimist fears that this is true.
JAMES BRANCH CABEL

324 A pessimist is a man who looks both ways before crossing a one-way street. LAURENCE J PETER

Philosophy
325 Voltaire is reported to have said, *'Plus ça change, plus ça reste'* – meaning, 'There isn't much sense in doing anything these days.'* ROBERT BENCHLEY

326 Philosophy: unintelligible answers to insoluble problems. HENRY ADAMS

327 Philosophers are adults who persist in asking childish questions. ISIAH BERLIN

328 An open mind is all very well in its way, but it ought not be so open that there is no keeping anything in or out of it. SAMUEL BUTLER

329 Philosophers have always been happier in felling the orchards of their predecessors than in planting new ones.
LAMBERT JEFFRIES

330 Being a philosopher, I have a problem for every solution. ROBERT ZEND

331 *For there was never yet philosopher*
That could endure the toothache patiently.
WILLIAM SHAKESPEARE *(Much Ado About Nothing)*

Poets
332 A poet can earn much more money writing or talking about his art than he can by practising it. W H AUDEN

333 For a man to be a poet...he must be in love, or miserable. LORD BYRON

334 *It's hard to say why writing verse*
Should terminate in drink, or worse. A P HERBERT

335 Perhaps no person can be a poet, or can ever enjoy poetry, without a certain unsoundness of mind.
T B MACAULAY

Politeness (see also *Etiquette*)
336 I beg your pardon for calling on you in this informal way, but your house is on fire. MARK TWAIN (to new neighbour)

Politics
337 The whole art of political speech is to put *nothing* into it. It is much more difficult than it sounds.
HILAIRE BELLOC

338 As a politician never believes what he says, he is surprised when others believe him. CHARLES DE GAULLE

339 *Treason doth never prosper. What's the reason?*
If it doth prosper, none dare call it treason.
JOHN HARINGTON (1611-77)

340 We all know that Prime Ministers are wedded to the truth, but like other married couples they sometimes live apart. SAKI

341 All governments are party governments. EDMUND BURKE

342 The minds of some of our own statesmen like the pupil of the human eye contract themselves the more, the stronger light there is shed upon them. THOMAS MORE

Poverty
343 People don't resent having nothing nearly as much as having too little. IVY COMPTON-BURNETT

344 There may be a pleasure in poverty, but it is a retrospective one. LAMBERT JEFFRIES

345 The truly poor man is not he who has little but he who wishes for more. SENECA

346 My mother's idea of economy was to take a bus to the Ritz. LADY TRUMPINGTON

Progress
347 What we call progress is the exchange of one nuisance for another nuisance. HAVELOCK ELLIS

348 Nothing is ever done in this world until men are prepared to kill one another if it is not done.
GEORGE BERNARD SHAW

Psychology/psychiatry
349 Anyone who goes to a psychiatrist ought to have his head examined. SAM GOLDWYN

350 Many who go into [psychoanalysis] do so in order to overcome their own neurosis. PROFESSOR ERNEST JONES

Quotations

351 Padding with quotes is usually done when the author is afraid to present his own opinion or else is anxious to show that he is widely read. PHILIP BONEWITS

352 We pay much more attention to a wise passage when it is quoted than when we read it in the original author. P G HAMERTON

353 When in doubt, ascribe all quotations to Bernard Shaw. NIGEL REES

354 I often quote myself: it adds spice· to the conversation. GEORGE BERNARD SHAW

Rail travel

355 I pick the loser every time. If you ever see me in a queue at the railway booking-office, join the other one, because there'll be a chap at the front of mine who's trying to send a rhinoceros to Tokyo. J BASIL BOOTHROYD

356 For safety in a train take a centre carriage and a right-hand seat; in case of a coming collision throw yourself either into the rack or under the seat. STRAND MAGAZINE

Religion

357 The Bible is like the poor: we have it always with us but we know very little about it. SAMUEL BUTLER

358 I dared to ask my history master, Ruppy Headlam, for his views on a future life. He replied, 'Doubtless I shall inherit eternal bliss, but I prefer not to discuss so depressing a topic.' CHRISTOPHER HOLLIS

359 Half the rules seemed to forbid things he had never heard of; and the other half forbade things he was doing every day and could not imagine not doing. C S LEWIS

360 Musical comedy songs have always tended to spread a little more happiness than the average hymn. ARTHUR MARSHALL

361 A little girl had just been assured that God could do anything. 'Then, if he can do anything, can he make a stone so heavy that he can't lift it?' A A MILNE

362 O Lord, thou knowest I have nine houses in the City of London and have lately purchased an estate in Essex. I beseech thee to preserve the counties of Middlesex and Essex from fires and earthquakes. JOSHUA WARD (d. 1761)

School
363 To my father a school was not a seat of learning but a noisy detention compound to which children were sent for long periods of the year in order to be removed from under their parents' feet. R F DELDERFIELD

364 I used to visit the lavatories when I was frightened, and as I was frightened most of the time I got to know the lavatories pretty well. LUDOVIC KENNEDY

365 You can't expect a boy to be depraved until he has been to a good school. SAKI

366 I liked Eton, except in the following respects: for work and games, for boys and masters. OSBERT SITWELL

Science
367 The real joy of science is escaping from all the ordinary pressures of existence into a world where you can be completely happy doing something quite absorbing and largely useless. J BASIL BOOTHROYD

368 If an experiment works, something has gone wrong. *MURPHY'S LAW*

Seaside

369 *There's sand in the porridge and sand in the bed,*
And if this is pleasure we'd sooner be dead!
NOËL COWARD

Secrets

370 Stolen waters are sweet, and bread eaten in secret is
pleasant. *PROVERBS* ix, 17

371 He that hath a secret should not only hide it, but hide
that he has it to hide. THOMAS CARLYLE

Sex

372 My husband believes that a Casanova provides a
useful social service, claiming that the best women, like
Rolls-Royces, should be delivered to the customer fully
run in. JILLY COOPER

373 The difference between sex for money and sex for
free is that sex for money usually costs a lot less. BRENDAN
FRANCIS

374 Her dachshund, she said, was oversexed. Could I
please do something to damp his ardour. Well, indeed I
could. I recommended the remedy that has damped male
ardour since time began. I found him a wife.
BUSTER LLOYD-JONES

375 Contraceptives should be used on every conceivable
occasion. SPIKE MILLIGAN

376 Whoever named it necking was a poor judge of
anatomy. GROUCHO MARX

377 My life is an open book – all too often open at the
wrong page. MAE WEST

378 When I'm good I'm very, very good, but when I'm
bad I'm better. MAE WEST

Shakespeare

379 I don't think I should want to know Shakespeare. I know him as well as I want by knowing his plays.
JONATHAN MILLER

380 He had read Shakespeare and found him weak in chemistry. H G WELLS

Sin

381 The only difference between the saint and the sinner is that every saint has a past and every sinner has a future.
OSCAR WILDE

Smoking

382 Tobacco, divine, rare, super-excellent tobacco, which goes far beyond all their panaceas, potable gold and philosopher's stones, a sovereign remedy to all diseases.
ROBERT BURTON (17th century clergyman and author) [But see below.]

383 But as it is commonly abused by most men, which take it as tinkers do to ale, 'tis a plague, a mischief, a violent purger of goods, land, health, hellish, devilish and damned tobacco, the ruin and overthrow of body and soul.
ROBERT BURTON (17th century clergyman and author)

384 I have made it a rule never to smoke more than one cigar at a time. MARK TWAIN

Speech

385 It is a fantasy that if you got lots of interesting and famous people together you would have every conversation possible. You wouldn't at all. You'd have envy, competition, rancour, and the whole thing would be very boring. JONATHAN MILLER

386 Val chatted away happily every moment of her waking day. She never said anything: just talked.
FRANK MUIR

387 *It is remarkable that they*
Talk most who have the least to say. MATTHEW PRIOR

388 Today's witty conversationalist is tomorrow's bore.
ANNE SCOTT-JAMES

389 He has occasional flashes of silence that make his conversation perfectly delightful. SYDNEY SMITH (of Macaulay)

390 I have often regretted my speech, never my silence.
PUBLILIUS SYRUS

Sport
391 The school sports day is a purgatory of tedium... Exciting finishes are rare oases in the desert of dullness, and always happen when I am looking at something else. BALAAM

392 Serious sport has nothing to do with fair play... It is war minus the shooting. GEORGE ORWELL

393 I play no outdoor games, except dominoes. I have sometimes played dominoes outside French cafés. OSCAR WILDE

Stealing
394 Ambidextrous: able to pick a pocket with either hand. AMBROSE BIERCE

395 A burglar who respects his art always takes his time before he takes anything else. O HENRY

Stupidity
396 Idiot: a member of a large and powerful tribe whose influence on human affairs has always been dominant.
AMBROSE BIERCE

397 'I simply cannot bear fools.'
'Apparently your mother did not have the same difficulty.' DOROTHY PARKER

Success

398 The toughest thing about success is that you've got to keep on being a success. IRVING BERLIN

399 Success is the one unpardonable sin against one's fellows. AMBROSE BIERCE

400 For one person spoilt by success, a thousand are spoilt by failure. LAMBERT JEFFRIES

401 Nothing recedes like success. WALTER WINCHELL

Superstition

402 Faith is what we believe in but cannot prove. Superstition is what other people believe in but cannot prove. LAMBERT JEFFRIES

403 Loch Ness has not got a monster in it, but the locals are keeping the fact quiet. FRANK MUIR

Teachers

404 Every schoolmaster knows that for every one person who wants to teach there are approximately thirty who don't want to learn. W C SELLAR and R J YEATMAN

Television and radio

405 I'll believe in colour television when I see it in black and white. SAM GOLDWYN

406 The main and most glorious achievement of television is that it is killing the art of conversation. If we think of the type of conversation television is helping to kill, our gratitude must be undying. GEORGE MIKES

407 He was a shortish, middle-aged man with a look of uneasy jauntiness, like those minor relatives who swarm on at the end of *This Is Your Life*. DENIS NORDEN

408 Television is entertainment that flows like tap-water.
DENNIS POTTER

409 These days a star is anyone who can hold a microphone. HARRY SECOMBE

Temptation
410 'You ought not to yield to temptation.'
'Well *somebody* must or the thing becomes absurd.'
ANTHONY HOPE

411 I can resist anything except temptation. OSCAR WILDE

412 I generally avoid temptation, unless I can't resist it.
MAE WEST

Tennis
413 As an irascible veteran, Gardnar Mulloy once removed his glasses and offered them to an erring linesman. PAUL METZLER

414 In the right-hand court I use the American service, which means that I never know till the last moment which side of the racket is going to hit the ball. A A MILNE

Theatre
415 The audience was tremendously fashionable, and, for the first part of the play [*Bitter Sweet*], almost as responsive as so many cornflour blancmanges. NOËL COWARD

416 Back in ten minutes – Godot. (Sign in greenroom gents' lavatory.)

417 It is well understood by every dramatist that a late-dining audience needs several minutes of dialogue before it recovers from its bewilderment at finding itself in a theatre. A A MILNE

Thinking

418 Brain: an apparatus with which we think that we think. AMBROSE BIERCE

419 The trouble with the person who always says what he thinks is that he *talks* more than he thinks.
LAMBERT JEFFRIES

420 When we all think alike, no one is thinking.
WALTER LIPPMANN

421 Nothing is so firmly believed as what we least know.
MICHEL DE MONTAIGNE

Tragedy

422 There are two tragedies in life. One is not to get your heart's desire; the other is to get it. GEORGE BERNARD SHAW

423 When the gods wish to punish us, they answer our prayers. OSCAR WILDE

Travel

424 It's easier to find a travelling companion than to get rid of one. PEG BRACKEN

425 The great question about abroad is, is it worth getting there? ROSE MACAULAY

426 I love the Old Travellers...for their witless platitudes; for their supernatural ability to bore; for their startling, their brilliant, their overwhelming mendacity. MARK TWAIN

Truth

427 I don't mind lies, but I hate inaccuracy. SAMUEL BUTLER

428 There is probably no popularly-received belief which is absolutely true. R T GOULD

429 Truth wears a different face to everybody. J R LOWELL

430 Truth is never pure, and rarely simple. OSCAR WILDE

Tyranny
431 Bad laws are the worst sort of tyranny. EDMUND BURKE

432 The best government is a benevolent tyranny, modified by an occasional assassination. VOLTAIRE

Wales
433 The land of my fathers. And my fathers can have it. DYLAN THOMAS

434 I thought I was coming home when I came back to Cardiff. But Cardiff is just a big provincial city with a lot of Welsh people in it. GWYN WILLIAMS

War
435 As long as war is regarded as wicked, it will always have its fascination. When it is looked upon as vulgar, it will cease to be popular. OSCAR WILDE

436 The way to win an atomic war is to make certain it never starts. GENERAL OMAR BRADLEY

437 You can't say civilisations don't advance... In every war they kill you a new way. WILL ROGERS

Weather
438 Rain is accepted by the Londoner as an inescapable fact of life, like shaving, contraception and income tax. LEN DEIGHTON

439 Who wants to be foretold the weather? It is bad enough when it comes, without our having the misery of knowing about it beforehand. J K JEROME

440 If December passes without snow, we indignantly demand to know what has become of our good, old-fashioned winters and talk as if we had been cheated out

of something we had bought and paid for; and when it does snow our language is a disgrace to a Christian nation.
J K JEROME

441 If I were running the world I would have it rain only between 2am and 5am. Anyone out then ought to get wet.
W L PHELPS

Women/wives

442 I have always thought that every woman should marry, and no man. DISRAELI

443 All women become like their mothers – that is their tragedy. No man does – that is his. OSCAR WILDE

444 Women are meant to be loved – not understood. OSCAR WILDE

445 I expect that woman will be the last thing civilised by man. GEORGE MEREDITH

446 I have prejudices about women. I do not like to see them eat. LORD BYRON

447 What is a woman? Only one of Nature's agreeable blunders. HANNAH COWLEY

448 Modern drugs are wonderful. They enable a wife with pneumonia to nurse her husband through 'flu.
FAITH HINES and PAM BROWN

449 *Little dabs of powder,*
Little smears of paint,
Make a woman's wrinkles
Look as if they ain't. HELEN MAY

450 When women go wrong, men go right after them.
MAE WEST

451 *The English woman is so refined,*
She has no bosom and no behind. STEVIE SMITH

Writing

452 After you've praised a writer's last work, the conversation rather lags. W H AUDEN

453 If the tutors of correspondence courses gave discouraging advice, their purses would grow thin, and they might themselves be driven to write for a living. BALAAM

454 To give an accurate and exhaustive account...would need a far less brilliant pen than mine. MAX BEERBOHM

455 It took me fifteen years to discover I had no talent for writing, but I couldn't give it up because by that time I was too famous. ROBERT BENCHLEY

456 When writers meet they do not usually talk about writing: they talk about money. PATRICK SKENE CATLING

457 When two people are collaborating on the same book, each believes he gets all the worries and only half the royalties. AGATHA CHRISTIE

458 Unprovided with original learning, unformed in the habits of thinking, unskilled in the arts of composition, I resolved to write a book. EDWARD GIBBON

459 Sir, no man but a blockhead ever wrote except for money. SAMUEL JOHNSON

460 You will never write a good book until you have written some bad ones. GEORGE BERNARD SHAW

461 I write plays because dialogue is the most respectable way of contradicting myself. TOM STOPPARD

Words
462 The two most beautiful words in the English language are 'Cheque enclosed'. DOROTHY PARKER

Youth
463 Youth is a blunder; manhood a struggle; old age a regret. DISRAELI

23

Index of Quotations

Reference numbers shown are those of the quotation, not the page.
A name in capitals denotes the author of a quotation.

GOULD, R (428)
Government (135), (432)
Graves (140)
Great men (195)
Greatness (3)
GREEN, M (113), (286)
Green thinking (55), (102)
GUICCIARDINI, F (190)
Habits (107)
Hair (215)
HALIFAX, MARQUIS OF (245)
HAMERTON, P (352)
Handwriting (148), (322)
Happiness (218), (219)
HARDY, T (169), (279)
HARINGTON, J (339)
HAY, I (131)
HAZLITT, W (234)
Head, losing (139)
Healing (145)
Health (250)
Healthy eating (188)
Heart's desire (422)
Heaven (56)
HELLER, J (271)
HELPMAN, R (80)
HENRY, O (395)
Hepburn, K (256)
HERBERT, A (267), (334)
HERFORD, O (162)
Heritage (217)
Heroes (309)
HERRIOT, J (147)
HINES, F (237), (448)
History (216), (217)
HITCHCOCK, A (116)
Holiday (221)
Holidays (220)
HOLLIS, C (358)

Home (180)
Honesty (222-226)
Honour (65)
HOOD, T (127)
HOPE, B (39), (410)
Horses (227), (228)
Hospitality (229)
Hotels (230)
Housework (236), (237)
HOWARTH, R (188)
HUBBARD, E (214), (293)
HUGHES, S (308)
HUGO, V (44)
HULL, R (287)
Human race (232)
Humanity (235)
Humour (238-240)
HUNT, L (30), (56), (81),
  (187)
Hunting (241-243)
Husbands (245), (246),
  (448)
Hustling (2)
HUXLEY, A (72), (221)
HUXLEY, J (16)
Hymns (360)
Hypochondria (17)
Hypocrisy (14)
Idiot (396)
Idleness (90), (91)
Ignoramus (247)
Ignorance (247), (248)
Illness (249), (250)
Imagination (251), (252)
Inaccuracy (427)
Indifference (50)
Indiscretion (279)
Influence (396)
Ingratitude (52)

211

24
The Jokes

Telling jokes is an art. It is best left to stand-up comics. *Weaving* a joke or amusing story into your speech, in a way that makes it sound like a natural component, however, is by far the best way to deal with them.

You will find in the following pages a host of quips and longer pieces, some with the potential for generating belly-laughs, some that may induce pleasant, knowing chortles. Don't think that all jokes and stories have to be uproariously, side-splittingly funny.

Don't feel you have to stick slavishly to the wording. Adapt the joke to the situation. But, even if the rest of your speech is being delivered from brief notes, do write out the punchlines of the jokes in full. It would be a shame to get so far and forget the punchline or make a hash of it.

A word of warning: almost every joke has the potential for offending *somebody*. You will find odd pieces of advice at the start of some of the categories. But a general piece of advice is: take care. Determine what type of audience you're speaking to. Don't tell gleeful stories about Herod the Great when doing the opening speech for the mother-and-baby competition. Especially if it's near Christmas.

Also, it is easy to be offensively sexist in a world in which women are quite properly exerting their right to be treated in every respect on an equal basis with men. Yes, there *are* some funny mother-in-law and wife jokes, which, when told warmly and with affection, can be funny and effective. But try now and again to turn the tables. Some stories can poke fun at men just as easily as they do at women.

The best way to use the jokes section, as with the quotations section, is to check the index. Cross-referencing is as exhaustive as we've been able to make it, making your job of finding a suitable quip, anecdote or quotation an easy one.

Accident

1   A man rushed into a pub in a rather agitated state. 'Does anybody here own a large black cat with a white collar?' he asks. No reply. 'Does anybody own a large black cat with a white collar?' he asks again, raising his voice even higher. Still no answer. 'Oh, dear,' he mutters. 'Must have run over the vicar.'

Acting

2   Timothy desperately wanted to be a famous actor and always believed in trying to 'live' any parts he was asked to play. When he was invited to audition for the part of Abraham Lincoln in a new play, he read all about Lincoln. He researched Lincoln's background for weeks and then dressed to look exactly like him – black hat, black cloak, red sash and large black boots. After admiring himself in a mirror, he set off for the audition. He didn't get the part – but on the way home he was assassinated.

Advertising

3   The tea manufacturers wanted a new advertising gimmick, so the senior creative artist at their agency decided to go to Rome to see if he could persuade the Pope to make a TV commercial. The Pope gave the adman an audience and he made his request.

'We'll give you a hundred thousand pounds for a ten-second ad. All you do is say, "Give us this day our daily tea".'

'I'm sorry,' replied the Pope, 'but I cannot do as you request.'

'*Five* hundred thousand,' offered the adman.

'I'm afraid not,' said the Pope solemnly.

'All right. One million pounds. And that's our very last offer.'

But still the Pope refused to make the commercial and the adman left. On the way home the adman turned to his secretary and said, 'That's odd. I mean, the Pope refusing to do a commercial for tea. I wonder how much the bread people are paying him?'

Artificial insemination

4   All the farmers in the area were going over to artificial insemination for their herds – all, that is, except Walter Mangelwurzel. Walter refused to have anything to do with such new-fangled ideas, but one day the vet decided to convince him of the advantages of artificial insemination for his cows.

Well, Walter stopped harnessing his wife to the plough to listen to the vet, and he was pleased with what he heard and agreed to give the idea a try.

That afternoon, the vet returned and said, 'Did you put that bucket of hot water and a towel in the cowshed as I asked?'

'Yes,' says Walter, 'and there's a hook behind the door you can hang your trousers on.'

Babies

5   There were two babies in the pram. One baby turned to the other baby and said, 'Are you a little girl or a little boy?'

'I don't know,' giggled the other baby.

'I can tell,' said the first baby, and he dived beneath the bedclothes and then resurfaced. 'You're a girl and I'm a boy,' he announced proudly.

'That was clever,' said the baby girl. 'How could you tell?'

'Easy! You've got pink bootees and I've got blue ones.'

6   'He's just like his father.'
'I know – bald, sleepy and uneducated.'

Banking

7   A young woman went into a bank and asked to withdraw some money.

'Can you identify yourself?' asked the clerk.

The young woman opened her handbag, took out a mirror, looked into it and said, 'Yes, it's me all right.'

Bees

8   Why do bees hum? Because they don't know the words.

Belch

9   'How *dare* you belch in front of my wife?'

'Why? Was it her turn?'

Belief

10   Have you heard about the insomniac agnostic dyslexic who lies awake every night wondering if there really is a dog?

Biblical

(Jokes about religion, like others' cultures and ethnicity, can cause offence if handled badly or told to the wrong sort of audience, so take care.)

11   Eve was so jealous of Adam that when he came home each night she used to count his ribs.

12   When God had finally formulated his Ten Commandments, he approached all the various races and tribes of people on the earth and asked if they would like them. The Arabs were a bit cautious and asked, 'What do these commandments say?'

'Well,' said God, 'one of them says, "Thou shalt not steal." '

'But that's no good,' replied the Arabs. 'We can't possibly take them, as we earn so much of our living by plundering travellers.'

God then asked the French if *they* would take his

commandments. But they, too, wanted to know what they commanded. When God got to 'Thou shalt not commit adultery', the French stopped him, shaking their heads sadly.

'We don't think these commandments, especially that one, are suitable for us.'

God offered his commandments to many other peoples, but they all rejected them as being unsuitable to their particular way of life. Eventually, in desperation, God approached the Jews.

'How much do they cost?' asked Moses.

'They're completely free of charge,' God replied.

'Good,' said Moses. 'In that case, we'll take all ten.'

13   British Rail is mentioned in the book of Genesis, you know. It says there that God created every creeping thing.

14   The Sunday School teacher who'd been telling his class the story of Jonah and the whale finished by asking them what lesson they thought the story taught.

One little boy put up his hand. 'Please, sir,' he piped, 'that you can't keep a good man down.'

Birth
15   We were a bit worried when I was [or my wife was] expecting our sixth child. You see, we'd just read in the paper that every sixth child born in the world is Chinese.

Boasting
16   A young man was loudly lamenting to everyone in the bar that his doctor had ordered him to give up half his sex life.

'Which half are you going to give up?' asked a bored listener. 'Talking about it – or thinking about it?'

17   A man who had been boasting of his achievements for what seemed like hours at last concluded with, 'I'm a self-made man! That's what I am: a self-made man!'

One of the company, stifling a yawn, observed in a

bored voice, 'Really, old man! Then you gave up work too soon!'

Builders

(Jokes about people's mental capacity can be tricky and may cause offence if there's a member of your audience who has a relative with a mental or psychiatric problem. The word 'lunatic' is so outrageous and little used these days that it is probably the safest word to use in story-telling.)

18   Three lunatics were working on a building site, supposedly digging a trench. After a few hours the foreman came along and was surprised to find one of the men digging furiously, while the other two were standing motionless, their shovels in the air, claiming they were both lamp-posts. The foreman sacked the two men immediately and told them to go home. But the man in the trench also stopped work.

'It's all right,' said the foreman. 'I haven't fired you. You were working very well, so carry on.'

The man asked, 'But how the hell do you expect me to work in the dark?'

Burglaries

19   You can never be too careful. A recently married couple I know received by post two tickets for an Andrew Lloyd Webber musical. Accompanying them was a card saying, 'Guess who from!'

So they went to the concert, having spent the day pondering over who might have sent them the kind invitation.

When they got home they found that their house had been burgled and all their wedding presents and other valuables stolen. On the mantlepiece there was a card, similar to that which had accompanied the tickets. On it was written, 'Now you *know* who from.'

Cannibals

20　The cannibal drank a lot of soup from an enormous cooking pot, then turned to his friend, belched and said, 'I've had a bellyful of your mother.'

21　'I don't think much of your wife.'
　　'Never mind – just eat the vegetables.'

22　A clever cannibal was very successful in the heart of the jungle when he set up a crematorium and sold peopleburgers.

23　The cannibal came home to find his wife chopping up snakes and a very small man. 'Oh, no!' he groaned. 'Not snake-and-pygmy pie again!'

24　'And this soup contains wholesome, health-giving vitamin Bill Brown.'

Carpentry

25　How can you easily decide whether to use a screw or a nail when doing carpentry? Drive in a nail – and if the wood splits you should have used a screw.

Cars

26　I really bought a baby car – it doesn't go anywhere without a rattle.

27　Henry was trying to sell his battered old car for £900. His friend, Tom, said he would pay 10% less than the price Henry was asking for it. But Henry wasn't very good at figures, so he said he'd think about Tom's offer. That evening, when he was in his usual bar, Henry asked the barmaid, 'If I offered you nine hundred quid less ten percent, what would you take off?'
　　The barmaid hesitated slightly, then replied, 'Everything except my earrings.'

28　I've got a two-tone car: black and rust.

Cats

29   The vet had just supervised the delivery of a litter of kittens to the old lady's cat.

'I just don't know how it could've happened,' said the old woman. 'Tibbles is never allowed out and no other cats are ever allowed into the house.'

'But what about him?' the vet asked, pointing to a large tomcat sitting in an armchair.

'Oh, don't be silly,' the woman replied. 'That's her brother.'

Cause and effect

30   An old school chum of mine – bit of a swot in class, always had his nose in books and test-tubes – anyway, he's a professor now at Cambridge and has devoted his entire life to arachnid research. A few weeks ago he was about to make a major announcement to the world. He'd written an article for *Nature* magazine, had the press there, loads of experts, the lot. When everybody was seated, my pal the prof strode into the room and put a spider on a table in front of him and commanded it to walk three paces forward. To the astonishment of the audience, it did as it was told.

'Now take three paces backwards,' said the prof. The spider did so. Amazing.

Then he pulled the spider's legs off and put it down on the table and said, 'Now take three paces to the left.'

The spider didn't move. Just sat there. So the professor looks up above his half-moon glasses at the audience, raises an eyebrow and says, 'You see. That proves that when you pull off the legs of a spider it goes deaf.'

Chemists

31   Customer: 'I'd like to buy some poison for mice.'
Chemist: 'Have you tried Boots?'
Customer: 'I want to poison 'em, not kick 'em to death!'

224

Christianity

32 A shipwrecked sailor had been drifting about on a raft for weeks, when one day he suddenly sighted land. As he came closer to the shore, he saw a group of people on the beach building a gallows.

'Thank God,' he sighed. 'A Christian country.'

Cinemas

33 A man was making loud groaning noises during a sexy love scene on the screen. He soon had other members of the audience around him hissing for him to be quiet. But he continued to moan and groan. They eventually called the manager.

'Get up!' the manager commanded.

'Oooooooh! Aaaaaaaagh!' the man went on, louder than ever.

'Where are you from?' the manager demanded.

'Fr... From...fr...' groaned the man, '...from th...the balcony.'

34 During the interval the house lights wouldn't come on, and the cinema audience were groping around in the dark. Then the Chinese cinema manager came onto the stage, barely visible against the curtain.

'I'd like you all to raise your hands,' he told the audience. Incredulous, but happy for something to relieve the boredom, every member of the audience raised his or her hands into the air.

Miraculously, all the house lights came on. There were gasps of surprise and shouts of, 'How did you do that?'

'Old Chinese proverb,' said the manager. 'Many hands make light work.'

35 A young girl was complaining to her friend in the cinema foyer after the movie.

'It was terrible. I had to change seats five times.'

'Why?' asked her friend. 'Was some chap bothering you?'

'Yes – eventually.'

Conversations

36 'Why are you in such a hurry?'

'I'm off to the doctor. I don't like the look of my wife.'

'I'll come with you. I can't *stand* the sight of mine!'

37 'My wife speaks through her nose.'

'Why?'

'She's worn her mouth out.'

38 'I had to give up tap-dancing.'

'Why?'

'I kept falling into the sink.'

39 'That's a nice suit you're wearing. Who went for the fitting?'

40 'I didn't come here to be insulted.'

'Why? Where do you normally go?'

41 Judge in divorce case: 'Did you or did you not sleep with Mrs Smith on the night in question?'

'Not a wink, Your Honour.'

42 'Do you ever talk to your wife when you're making love?'

'Only if she telephones.'

43 'Do you smoke after making love?'

'Dunno. I've never looked.'

44 'Well, how do you find yourself these cold winter mornings?'

'Oh, you know, just throw back the blankets, and there I am.'

45 'Will the band play anything I request?'

'Certainly, sir.'

'Then tell them to play dominoes.'

Cows
46   The first time the little girl from the big city had ever seen a cow she thought it was a bull that had swallowed a glove.

Cowboys
47   'Who painted my horse blue?' yelled the angry cowboy as he entered the saloon.

Everyone was silent, and then a big, ugly mountain of a cowboy stood up, sauntered threateningly towards the first cowboy and admitted to having done the deed. As he looked up at the huge man towering above him, the newcomer said meekly, 'Oh. I only wanted to know when you're going to give it a second coat.'

48   The Lone Ranger and Tonto were riding along one morning when suddenly they saw five hundred Sioux chasing them. Galloping ahead as fast as they could they were astonished to find another five hundred Indians – Apaches, this time – racing towards them from the front, all dressed in war paint and giving excited war whoops.

The Lone Ranger slowed his horse to a gentle trot and turned to Tonto and said, 'Well, old friend, it looks as if this is going to be the finish for both of us.'

Tonto shook his head sadly and said, 'What do you mean, *both* of us, White Man?'

49   Two men were playing cards in the saloon. One of them thumped the table gleefully and said, 'I win!'

'What you got?' asked the other man.

'Four aces.'

'I'm afraid you don't win.'

'That's almost impossible,' said the first man. 'What cards have *you* got?'

'Two nines and a loaded gun.'

'Oh,' said the first man. 'You win. But how come you're so lucky?'

Deceit

50 In the divorce court the judge frowned and said, 'So, Miss Brown, you admit that you stayed in a hotel with this man?'

Woman: 'Yes, I do. But I couldn't help it. He deceived me.'

Judge: 'Really? How?'

Woman: 'Well he told the receptionist I was his wife.'

Diets

51 'The only way my Bill will lose weight is to have a leg off.'

52 I'm on a seafood diet. It's great: every time I see food I eat it.

Death

53 Pat was dying and the priest was giving him his last rites.

'Say after me,' said the priest, ' "I renounce the devil and all his works".'

Pat said not a word, so the priest repeated what he had just said. But Pat remained resolutely silent. The priest shook him and said, 'What's the matter? Can't you hear me?'

'Sure I can hear you, Father,' answered Pat. 'But don't you think this is the wrong time for me to antagonise anybody?'

Diving

54 A diver working 300 feet below the surface of the English Channel received a message from his ship, saying, 'Come up quick! We're sinking!'

Dentist

55 'Give it to me straight. How am I?'

'Well your teeth are fine. But your gums'll have to come out.'

Doctors

56 'Doctor, I'm worried about my wife. She thinks she's a bird.'

'Well you'd better tell her to come and see me.'

'I can't. She's flown south for the winter.'

57 A medical student was accompanying one of the consultants on his hospital rounds. Time after time, the student made a completely wrong diagnosis.

'Have you ever thought about taking up a different career?' asked the consultant. 'One where you wouldn't be fired for frequent mis-diagnoses? A government analyst, perhaps?'

58 Student doctor: 'Excuse me, sir, but there's some writing on this patient's foot.'

Famous surgeon: 'Ah, yes, that's a footnote.'

59 'Doctor, my hair keeps falling out. Have you got anything to keep it in?'

'How about a cardboard box?'

60 Patient: 'Doctor, have you got anything for my liver?'

Doctor: 'What about some onions?'

61 Patient: 'Got anything for my flat feet?'

Doctor: 'Have you tried a bicycle pump?'

62 Receptionist: 'The doctor's so funny, he'll soon have you in stitches.'

Patient: 'I hope not. I only came in for a check-up.'

63 Woman: 'I think I'm pregnant.'

Doctor: 'But I gave you the Pill.'

Woman: 'Yes, but it keeps falling out!'

64 'Doctor, I'm worried. I keep seeing pink striped crocodiles when I try to get to sleep.'

'Have you seen a psychiatrist?'
'No, only pink striped crocodiles?'

65 'Are you *sure* you've never been with a man, Miss Jones?'
'Yes, doctor. Never!'
'Are you quite sure? Bearing in mind that I've now examined the sample you sent, do you still say you've never had anything to do with men?'
'Quite sure, doctor. Can I go now?'
'Not just yet, Miss Jones.'
'Why not?'
'Because I'm awaiting the arrival of the Three Wise Men.'

66 The senior civil servant complained that he was unable to sleep.
'Oh, don't you sleep at night?' asked the doctor.
'Yes, I sleep very well at night. And I sleep quite soundly most of the mornings, too. But I find it very difficult to sleep in the afternoons as well.'

67 'And when my right arm's better, will I be able to play the trumpet?'
'Most certainly – you should be able to play it with ease.'
'Good, because I couldn't play it before.'

Dogs
68 'My dog plays chess with me.'
    'That's amazing. Intelligent pooch, eh?'
    'Nah. He's only won two games so far this evening.'

69 'I've just lost my dog.'
    'Why don't you put an ad in the paper?'
    'Don't be silly! My dog can't read.'

70 It was one of the strangest-looking dogs they had ever seen in the pub, and the regulars found it a great topic

of conversation.

Eventually one of them sidled over to the dog's owner and said, 'That's a stupid-looking dog you've got there. Can it fight?'

'Sure,' replied the owner.

'Well,' said the man, 'I bet you five pounds that my labrador can beat your dog.'

The owner accepted the bet and the labrador was led in to fight. After 22 seconds the labrador lay dead on the floor. The loser, looking down at his dead dog, shook his head sadly and said, 'Your dog certainly can fight. But I still think it's a funny-looking dog.'

'Yes,' agreed the owner. 'And it looked even funnier until I shaved its mane off.'

71 'My dog's got no tail.'
    'How do you know when it's happy?'
    'When it stops biting me.'

72 'Lovely bulldog you've got.'
    'It's not a bulldog. It was chasing a cat and ran into a wall.'

73 You can tell my neighbour's dog's a pedigree. It barks in a posh accent.

74 'I've had my dog put down.'
    'Was it mad?'
    'Well, it wasn't exactly pleased.'

Dolphins
75 Dolphins are so intelligent that within only a few weeks of being in captivity they can train a man to stand on the very edge of their pool and throw them fish three times a day.

Dreams
76 Simon was becoming worried about his ever-increasing weight. One day in his club he happened to

mention this to his friend, Peter.

'I can recommend a very good doctor,' said Peter. 'I owe my slimness all to Dr Frank Einstein. He's invented these marvellous pills I take.'

'It sounds amazing,' said Simon. 'But how do they work?'

'It's really psychological. Every night I take two of the pills just before going to sleep and I always dream about being on a South Sea island, surrounded by hordes of beautiful young native girls. And every day I chase them all around the island and when I wake up I seem to've sweated off a few ounces of surplus fat. It's incredible – and enjoyable!'

The following day Simon went to see Dr Einstein and begged him to give him the same tablets he was prescribing for Peter. The doctor agreed, and within a few weeks Simon was much thinner.

'How're you finding the treatment?' asked Dr Einstein, when Simon called in for his regular check-up.

'It's very good. But I do have one complaint.'

'Oh, and what's that?'

'The pills you gave my friend Peter made him have wonderful dreams about chasing young native girls all over an island. But all I seem to get is the same horrible nightmare – being chased all over the island by hungry cannibals. Why can't I have pleasant dreams like Peter?'

'Because,' replied the doctor, 'Peter's a private patient. You're National Health.'

Drinking

77 A Chinaman returning home from a holiday in Britain complained that we had peculiar customs. He said to a friend, 'They put a lump of sugar in a glass to make a drink sweet, then add lemon to make it sour. They put in gin to warm themselves up and then ice to make themselves cool. Afterwards they say, "Here's to you", but drink it themselves.'

232

Drunks

78 The landlord of a pub frequented by an extremely heavy drinker opened up one day and in walked a pink elephant, a green rhinoceros and several orange striped crocodiles.

'I'm sorry,' said the publican. 'I'm afraid he isn't in yet.'

79 A drunk came tottering out of a pub and found a man selling tortoises.

'How much?' asked the drunk.

'Only ten pounds each,' said the man.

'I'll take one,' said the drunk, and after he'd paid for the tortoise he took it and staggered off.

After 20 minutes the drunk came swaying up to the tortoise-seller and bought another tortoise before teetering off again.

Fifteen minutes later the drunk returned to the tortoise-seller.

'You know,' he said as he bought another tortoise, 'they've very expensive. But, by Jove, I really love your crunchy meat pies.'

Employers

80 Angry employer: 'Why are you late again this morning?'

Young typist: 'I overslept.'

Employer: 'You mean you sleep at home as *well!*'

81 At the company board meeting the chairman rose to make his speech.

'Who has been carrying on with my secretary?' he demanded.

This was met with silence.

'All right, then,' said the chairman, 'put it this way: who has *not* been carrying on with my secretary?'

Again there was silence, and then one man said, self-consciously, 'Me, sir.'

'Right,' said the chairman. '*You* sack her.'

233

Flying

82   The aeroplane was so old it even had an outside lavatory.

Food

83   Waiter: 'And how did you find the meat today, sir?'
Diner: 'Oh, I just lifted up a chip and there it was.'

84   A man decided to test a London restaurant's claim that it would serve anything a customer asked for.

'Elephant's ears on toast,' he demanded, and waited smugly. Eventually the head waiter came to his table and said, 'I do apologise, sir. We seem to've run out of bread.'

85   'Waiter, this plate's damp.'
'Yes, I know, sir, that's the soup.'

86   When I lived in lodgings my landlady kept some animals in the yard at the back of the house. The first day I was there, one of the chickens died, so we had chicken soup.

The next day, the pig died, so I was offered pork chops.
The following day, the duck died, so we had roast duck.
The next day my landlady's husband died – so I left.

Goldfish

87   The philosophical goldfish swam around in his bowl, then stopped for a few seconds and turned to his companion and asked, 'Do you believe in the existence of God?'

'Yes,' replied the second goldfish. 'Who else do you suppose changes our water?'

Grave-digger

88   The eminent surgeon was walking through his local churchyard and saw the grave-digger having a rest and drinking from a bottle of beer.

'Hey, you!' called the surgeon. 'How dare you laze about and drink alcohol in the churchyard! Get on with your job or I shall complain to the vicar.'

'I'd have thought you'd be the last person to complain,' said the grave-digger, 'bearing in mind all your blunders I've had to cover up.'

Hamster

89   The man was lonely so he went to the petshop and asked for an animal that would make a good companion for him, as he was allergic to birds and fish. The petshop owner recommended a hamster, so the man bought two hamsters, some hamster food and a cage.

But the following day he was back complaining that the two hamsters had died, and bought two more.

And the next day he was back again.

'Those two hamsters you sold me yesterday have died, too. I'll take your whole stock, and maybe then I'll find at least a few that'll survive, and maybe even breed and give me continued companionship and pleasure.'

So he took all the petshop's stock – all 58 of them.

But the following day the man was there again.

'All those hamsters have died. I don't want anything to do with animals ever again. They just seem to curl up an die just to spite me. But it seems a pity to waste all those hamster bodies. Is there anything you can suggest to do with them? It seems horrible to have to throw them in the dustbin.'

'Well,' said the petshop owner, 'if you mash them all up and boil them until you get a sort of gooey stuff, this makes excellent fertilizer for the garden.'

The man left the shop and went home to follow the petshop owner's instructions. But a week later the man was back in the petshop.

'I really must congratulate you on your excellent suggestion,' said the man. 'I did as you suggested with the hamster bodies and in no time at all I had seven gigantic beanstalks in my garden. In fact, they were so high I had to stick red lights on top of them to warn aeroplanes to keep away. That hamster mixture really is amazing stuff for beanstalks.'

'That's odd,' said the petshop owner. 'You usually get tulips from hamster jam.'

Hereafter
90   The small car pulled up to a sudden halt.

'Have you run out of petrol?' asked the girl, somewhat sarcastically.

'No, of course not, ' replied her young male companion.

'Then why have we stopped?'

'You will no doubt have noticed that we are parked in a secluded spot in the middle of this forest and miles from anywhere – so I thought you might like a discussion about the hereafter.'

'That's something new,' replied the girl. 'What do you mean?'

'Simple! If you're not hereafter what I'm hereafter, you'll be hereafter I've gone.'

Historical
91   Reporter: 'Apart from *that,* Mrs Lincoln, how did you enjoy the play?'

92   During the late 19th century some South American rebels had been rounded up by government forces. On the day set for their execution it was pouring with rain as the soldiers marched the rebels to the field where they were to be shot.

'It's not right that we should die,' complained one of the rebels.

'Shut up!' snapped a soldier. 'Think yourself lucky you don't have to walk back to prison in this weather.'

93   With the Gaul having been captured, Caeser decided to put him in the arena to fight. First he was matched against a hungry lion, but the Gaul calmly picked up the animal as it rushed towards him, whirled it around in the air by its tail and then smashed in its head.

The promoters of the fight were annoyed, so the Gaul was given a choice. Either fight a pack of lions or enter into combat with their best gladiator.

But the promoters knew the audience wanted to see blood – the blood of the Gaul – so, as a slight handicap, the man was buried up to his neck in sand. The gladiator approached, drew his six-foot-long sword, raised it above the Gaul's head – to an enormous cheer from the audience – then brought it down.

But the Gaul moved his head to one side so the sword hit the ground.

The crowd rose to their feet, jeering and shouting, 'Fight fair, you coward!'

94 Paul Revere came thundering up to a small farmhouse during his historic ride from Boston to Lexington. The young farmer's wife came to the door.

'Get ya husband,' yelled Revere. 'We gotta fight the English.'

'My husband ain't home,' she replied, trembling.

'Get ya sons and kinsfolk,' he yelled.

'Ain't got no sons nor kinsfolk.'

'Ain't *no*body at home?'

'Nope.'

'Well I'll be! Can I interest you in buyin' some insurance?'

Hollywood
95 A Hollywood props department manager answered his phone only to hear the director bawl at him, 'Why haven't you got me the full-scale mock-up of the inside of the Titanic, like I asked for yesterday? And where are the fifty-six stuffed penguins I asked for this morning? How the hell do you expect me to make a film about King Canute without the props I asked for?'

'But...but...' stammered the props manager.

'Don't "but...but..." me!' roared the director. 'Nobody on this movie seems to care about accuracy and realism except me. Now get me those props or...'

'But if you keep shouting all the time,' soothed the props manager, 'you'll get ulcers and...'

'I don't *get* ulcers,' roared the director. 'I *give* 'em!'

Hospital

96   Nurse: 'Well, Mr Mitchell, you seem to be coughing much more easily this morning.'

Mr Mitchell, groaning in his bed: 'That's because I've been practising all night.'

Hotels

97   It was one o'clock in the morning and the manager of the hotel had just been woken by a frantic phone call from a little old lady.

'Come quickly! Oh, please come quickly!' she pleaded. 'I can see a naked man from my window.'

The manager hastily dressed and rushed up to the old lady's room. He found her pointing to a block of flats opposite her bedroom. But all the manager could see was the naked *top* half of a young man.

'But my dear lady,' he said, 'the young man opposite is surely only preparing for bed. And how can you possibly be offended by him? The man may not be completely naked.'

'Oh yes he is,' cried the little old lady.

'But how can you possibly know?'

'If you stand on the wardrobe...and look through these binoculars...'

98   The young woman was lying naked, face down, on the roof of her expensive hotel, sunbathing. Suddenly the manager came up to her, coughed slightly, then said, 'Excuse me, madam, but this is hardly the place for nudity.'

'Why not?' asked the young woman. 'There's nobody else up here – and I *am* lying face down.'

'Quite,' said the manager. 'But you're lying on the skylight over the dining room and it is now lunchtime.'

Hypochondria

99   Seen on a tombstone: 'See, I *told* you I was ill!'

Irishmen

(Jokes about people's cultures and ethnicity are fraught with problems. Make sure of your audience, and never aim to insult. Gentle fun is one thing; offence is quite another. The most effective way of telling these jokes is against oneself. Jews, note, are always quite self-deprecatory, and amusingly so.)

100 Three Irishmen were walking along a road when a young man in a battered sports car ran over them. He got out of his car and buried them in a field. Then, filled with remorse, he went to a police station to report what he had done.

'I'm terribly sorry, officer,' he said, 'but I've just run over three Irishmen and so I buried them in a field.'

'Are you sure they were dead?' asked the policeman.

'Well,' said the young man, 'two said they weren't – but you know what liars Irishmen are.'

101 An Irishman was stopped at the customs checkpoint after returning from a holiday on the Continent.

'What's this in the bottle?' asked the customs officer, taking out a large bottle from the Irishman's suitcase.

'Oh,' said the Irishman, 'that's only holy water from Lourdes.'

'Hmmm!' muttered the customs officer as he took the top off the bottle and sniffed the liquid inside. Then he tasted some of it.

'It looks, smells and tastes very much like whisky to me, sir.'

'Glory be!' replied the Irishman. ''Tis another miracle!'

102 It was pouring with rain and the old man fell down, dying, in the gutter. A man saw this and rushed up to help.

'What can I do? Where do you live? What's your name?' asked the man.

'Seamus O'Reilly,' replied the old man. 'I'm dying. There's nothing you can do to help.'

'But shall I fetch the priest?'

'No, fetch the rabbi.'

'Did I hear you right?' asked the man. 'With a name like Seamus O'Reilly and an accent like yours, you want me to fetch the rabbi and not the priest?'

'Yes,' replied the old man. 'I wouldn't bring the priest out on a night like this.'

103 It was the annual meeting of the International Brotherhood of Space Scientists in the year 2097.

'We are preparing to send a rocket to Pluto,' announced the Americans, proudly. 'It will have six men on board and will stay on Pluto for a whole month before making the long trip back to Earth.'

'That's nothing,' scoffed the Russians. 'We are almost ready to launch our spaceship containing two hundred men and women to start the first colony on Uranus.'

'Our country can beat you both,' said the Irish scientist. 'We're going to send a rocket straight to the sun.'

'Don't be silly,' said the American and Russian scientists. 'The rocket will melt before it gets there.'

'No it won't,' said the Irish scientist. 'We're sending it up at night.'

Jobs

104 A girl who was being interviewed for a job was asked if she had any special qualifications or abilities.

'Oh, yes,' she replied. 'I've won prizes for crosswords and limericks.'

'That's very good,' said the employer, 'but we want someone who's clever during office hours.'

The girl sat up and looked at the boss and said, 'But I *did* them during office hours.'

Journalists

105 A prayer: Forgive us our press-passes.

Jews

106 Levi went to the Jewish burial ground and asked the

rabbi if he could bury a cat. The rabbi was horrified.

'You, a good Jew, want to bury a cat in the graveyard?' he said. 'Certainly not!'

'Then I can't give you the fifty thousand pounds it left the synagogue in its will,' replied Levi, sadly.

'Oh,' said the rabbi. 'Why didn't you say it was a Jewish cat?'

107 The newly opened shopping centre had three tailors – all with shops next to each other. As another coincidence, all three tailors – while unrelated to each other – were called Jacob Silverstein.

The first tailor put up a sign over his shop proclaiming, 'Jacob Silverstein – High Class Tailor.'

The second tailor, not to be outdone, put up a sign saying, 'Silverstein – the tailor of distinction.'

The third tailor put up a smaller notice above his shop, but it said, 'Silverstein's Tailors – Main Entrance.'

Landlord
108 The young man walked into the petshop and asked if he could buy 387 cockroaches, 18 rats and five mice.

'I'm sorry, sir, we can only supply the mice. But what did you want all the other creatures for?' asked the petshop manager.

'I was thrown out of my flat this morning,' replied the young man. 'And my landlord says I must leave the place exactly as I found it.'

Legal
109 The world-famous lawyer was holidaying on an expensive yacht when he fell overboard into a group of sharks. They declined to eat him out of professional courtesy.

110 The scene is a law court. The prosecution counsel faces the witness and rasps, 'Is it true you committed adultery on the 18th June in a snowstorm while riding on the roof of an automobile travelling at ninety miles an

hour through Slough with a one-legged dwarf waving a Union Jack?'

The young woman in the witness box looked straight at the barrister and said, calmly, 'What was the date again?'

Liars
111 'That damned wife of mine is a liar!'

'How do you know?'

'She said she spent the night with Clare.'

'So?'

'*I* spent the night with Clare.'

Lumberjack
112 James was a very old man and when he turned up at a Canadian lumberjacks' camp and asked if he could help in chopping down the trees no one would take him seriously.

'Let me show you how good I am,' begged the old man.

Eventually, the lumberjack boss got tired of the old man's whining and pleading and gave James an axe, saying, 'Don't try too hard, old man. We don't want you killing yourself.'

James took the axe and went over to the tallest trees near the camp. The lumberjacks were amazed to see the old man chop away at the tree with enormous speed, and within only a few minutes the tree was lying on the ground.

'That's amazing!' said the lumberjack boss. 'Where did you learn to chop trees down like that?'

'In the Sahara,' replied the old man.

'But there aren't any trees in the Sahara,' said the boss.

'Yup, I know,' said the old man with a wry smile. 'Pretty good goin', huh?'

Marriage
113 Man: 'In your sermon this morning, vicar, you said it was wrong for people to profit from other people's mistakes. Do you really agree with that?'

Vicar: 'Yes. Of course I do.'

Man: 'In that case, will you consider refunding the twenty pounds I paid you for marrying me to my wife seven years ago?'

114 My wife's had so many facelifts that every time she smiles she pulls her knickers up.

115 My wife's had her face lifted so many times that now they have to lower her body.

116 My neighbour was fed up of being left alone at night by her husband. It was the same every night before he went to the pub. He'd say, 'Good-bye, mother of four.'

Well, she got more and more fed up of this ritual. One night he left with the usual greeting, 'Good-bye, mother of four.'

So she replied, 'Good-bye, father of two.'

He didn't go out again.

117 My wife said casually one day that the woman next door had a coat exactly like hers. Half taking the hint, I said, 'I suppose that means you want a new coat?' Always the clever negotiator, she said, 'Well, I suppose it would be cheaper than moving to a new house.'

118 I wouldn't say my husband was stupid, but when he went to a mindreader she gave him his money back.

119 The married couple arrived late one night at a hotel, only to be told by the manager, 'I'm sorry, but we're almost full up. All I have to offer you is the bridal suite.'

'But we've been married fifty years,' said the man.

'So?' said the manager. 'I could let you have the ballroom – but you wouldn't have to dance.'

120 Two young women were talking. One said to the other, 'My husband tricked me into marrying him. Before we got engaged he said he was a multi-millionaire.'

The other one replied, 'But he *is* a multi-millionaire,

isn't he?'

'Yes, but he also said he was eighty-four and in poor health, and I've just found out he's only seventy-five and in perfect condition.'

Missionary

121 Things are not always what they seem. I had a friend who was a missionary, and on his travels he came to a small village where he decided to make a speech. It went something like this.

'You must love your enemies.'

And the native people raised their spears and shouted, 'Hussanga!'

Encouraged by this he went on, 'If a man should smite you, turn the other cheek.'

And the cry went up again: 'Hussanga!'

So he went on, 'Fighting is wrong. You must not fight.'

'Hussanga!'

So he went on, 'If a man asks for your coat, you should give him your shirt.'

'Hussanga!'

He was dead chuffed, emboldened, absolutely full of himself. He buttonholed one of the tribesmen as he began to leave the platform and said, 'I think my little speech went down quite well, don't you?'

'Hmm,' said the tribesman, and then pointed to the bottom of the platform steps and said, 'But mind you don't tread in the hussanga when you leave the platform.'

Mountaineering

122 A climber friend of mine tells the story of how he and a fellow climber called Bert were climbing a particularly difficult mountain, when Bert suddenly fell down a crevasse 500 feet deep. So my pal shouted down to him, 'You all right, Bert?'

Bert shouted back, 'I'm still alive, thank goodness!'

'Here,' said my friend, throwing down a rope. 'Tie this to your arms and I'll haul you up.'

'I can't grab it,' shouted Bert. 'My arms are broken.'

'Well fit it round your legs, then,' my friend told him.

'Can't do that, either,' came Bert's strained reply. 'My legs are broken.'

'Well put it in your mouth, then,' said my friend. This Bert duly did, and my pal started to haul him up: 490 feet, 400 feet, 200 feet, 100 feet, 50 feet. And then he called to him, 'You all right, Bert?'

And Bert's reply came, 'Yeh-h-h...h...h...h...'

Politicians

123 It's no use telling politicians to go to hell. They're trying to build it for us now.

124 The Tory politician's small son asked him, 'Daddy, what's a traitor?'

The father replied, rather pompously, 'It's someone who leaves our party and joins another.'

'And what's somebody who leaves another party and joins ours?' the little boy asked.

'Why, a convert,' replied the father.

125 A lifelong Socialist friend was on his deathbed and told me he was going to join the Tories.

'Have you gone mad?' I asked. 'You've been a Socialist all your life.'

'Well,' he said, almost coughing his last, 'I'd rather one of *that* lot died than one of us.'

126 It's amazing what they can do these days. A pal of mine went for a brain transplant, and was offered the choice of *two* brains. No kidding. 'You can have an architect's brain for ten grand or a politician's for a hundred grand.'

My friend was a bit perplexed.

'Is the politician's brain better than the architect's?' he asked.

'Nope,' said the doctor. 'It's just that the politician's brain has never been used.'

Reincarnation
127 I've believed in reincarnation ever since I was a young frog.

Religion
128 A lawyer who was fond of the good things in life was put to sit next to a hot-gospelling, temperance minister at an official dinner.

When the meal was over the waiter came up to him to ask what he'd have to drink with his coffee.

'Oh, a brandy, please,' said the lawyer.

The waiter then turned to the bigoted minister. 'And would you like a brandy, too, sir?'

'I'd rather commit adultery,' hissed the minister.

At once the lawyer retorted, 'Cancel my brandy. I didn't know there was a choice.'

Rhinoceros
129 Adam was naming the animals and Eve said, 'But why are you calling that big thing a rhinoceros?' So Adam replied, 'Because it *looks* like a rhinoceros, stupid!'

Romance
130 I heard one of the girls in our office talking about one of the chaps.

'I wouldn't go with Graham Smith if I were you,' she said. 'He's got a dirty mind.'

'Oh,' said the other girl. 'He seems such a nice, unassuming chap.'

'But he knows too many dirty songs. Really filthy, *vile* songs. Songs no one with an ounce of common decency would even *think* about,' said the first girl.

But the other girl protested. 'Surely he doesn't sing them in the office...I mean...in *front* of people...'

'No,' said the first girl. 'But he whistles them.'

(The next one could, depending on how well the groom can take a joke, be usefully used by the best man at a wedding.)

131 He asked her, 'Will you marry me?' – after he offered her this absolutely huge glittering engagement ring.

So she said, 'Oooh! Are they *real* diamonds?'

'I sincerely hope so,' he said. 'If not then I've just been swindled out of five quid.'

School

132 When I was a nipper the teacher asked me if I had any younger brothers or sisters who'd be coming to the school. I told my mum when I got home, and she said, 'Oh, that was nice of Miss Simmons to take an interest. What did she say when you told her you were an only child?'

'Nothing,' I said. 'She just took a deep breath and went *Phew!*'

133 Out of the mouths of babes and sucklings and all that... The other day I heard a couple of kids as they were walking home from school – only about five or six, they were – and the little boy said to the little girl, 'I found a contraceptive behind the radiator today.' And the little girl asked him, 'What's a radiator?'

Scotsmen

(Scots have an unwarranted reputation for being mean, but so have Jews and Yorkshire folk. Jokes that poke fun can be effective if told in the right way. Be careful, and tell them with warmth and some affection for the intended butt of the jokes. Any that concern the Scots' alleged meanness can just as easily be adapted to fit other groups, or, indeed, individual people you know and wish to poke friendly fun at.)

134 It was a Scottish wedding – the confetti was on elastic.

135 McTavish met his friend McIntyre on the street one day.

'I've just seen your Andrew,' he said. 'You told me he was studying to be an ear specialist. He just told me he's going to be a dentist. Why's he changed his mind?'

McIntyre gave a knowing smile. 'Oh, he changed his

mind when I told him that folk have 32 teeth but only two ears.'

136 The meanest Scotsman in the world was the one who fired a revolver on Christmas Eve outside the door of his home, and then came in and told his kids Santa Claus had committed suicide.

Sex

137 Out of the mouths of babes and sucklings... Kids learn quickly these days, don't they? We decided to tell our eldest lad about...you know, about the facts of life, but when it came to telling our youngest one we were a bit too embarrassed. So I called Simon in one day – he's the eldest one – and said, 'Simon, will you tell Jeremy about the birds and the bees?'

Simon said, 'Sure, dad.' And that was that. Until I overheard a conversation from their bedroom. Simon was saying, 'Jeremy, you know what Mummy and Daddy do in bed at night?' and Jeremy said, 'Yes.' And Simon said, 'Well it's just the same with the birds and the bees.'

Sin

138 'And what do we have to do before we can get forgiveness of sin?'

'Sin.'

Speeches

139 A politician was giving a speech, but he was so boring, pompous, long-winded and conceited that his audience were bored stiff. Suddenly a bullet whizzed past his ear.

'I see,' he said, showing the ultimate conceit, 'that a member of my audience has been so moved by my speech that he tried to commit suicide, but he needs an optician as the bullet has just whistled past my ear.'

140 An after-dinner speaker who was new to the art stood up and, having suitably saluted his audience, stopped, dumbfounded. Presently, however, he composed himself suffic-

iently to say, 'A few hours ago only the Lord and I knew what I was going to say. But now the Lord only knows...'

141 When a new Member of Parliament asked Mr Disraeli whether he should often take part in the debates, the Prime Minister told him that he thought not, that it was much better for the House to wonder why he *didn't* speak than why he did.

142 The after-dinner speeches and the introductions had all been far too long. Everyone was bored, including the last speaker, whose turn it now was. He got up and yawned.

'Ladies and gentlemen,' he began. 'I have been asked to give you an address.' He looked around his tired audience and went on, 'The address is Thirty-three Acacia Gardens, Richmond, and that's where I'm going now. Good night.'

143 A business executive had to make a speech at an important meeting attended by his business associates. He couldn't think of anything interesting to talk about, so in the end he decided to talk about sex.

When he arrived home his wife asked how his speech had gone. He replied that it had been a huge success.

'But what did you talk about?' she asked.

'Er, sailing,' he said.

A day or two later one of the man's business associates approached his wife at a cocktail party and said, 'Marvellous speech your husband gave the other night.'

'I know,' she replied. 'It's quite amazing really, because he's only tried it twice. The first time his hat blew off and the second time he was seasick.'

Spies

144 Before the changes in the former Soviet Union, Boris Goronivitch, the Russian sportsman and top secret agent, arrived in Swansea. His highly secret assignment was to contact a man called Jones at an address he had been given. But the address turned out to be a large block of flats, and five Joneses lived there, all on different floors.

So Boris took a chance with the man on the lowest of the five floors in question, and rapped on the door. As the door opened, Boris whispered, 'The wombats are migrating early this year.'

'Oh, no,' came a voice from within. 'I'm Jones the Milk. You want Jones the Spy – two floors up.'

145 During the days of the former Soviet Union, a British diplomat in Moscow was attending a dinner party at the Kremlin, and much to his enjoyment he found himself seated next to a beautiful young woman.

During the course of the meal the diplomat dropped his handkerchief, and gently stroked the ankle of the young woman as he picked it up. But this brought no response.

The diplomat soon dropped a fork, and gently patted the woman's knee when he picked up the fork. But the woman remained silent.

As he dropped his knife to the floor, the diplomat noticed the young woman scribbling hastily on the back of a menu. She handed him what she had written under the table, and the diplomat was somewhat surprised to read, 'When you reach your destination show no astonishment. Roger Barrington-Smythe, MI5.'

Success
146 'Success changes people,' observed the business tycoon, smiling sardonically. 'I'm now said to be eccentric, not impolite; witty, not infernally rude.'

Tax
147 The Inland Revenue's produced a new simplified return form. It has only two sections. A: how much do you earn? B: Send it.

Telephone
148 Bell invented the telephone, but he found it quite useless, and then hit on the idea of inventing the *second* telephone. This was wonderful – until he invented the *third* telephone, called the second and found it engaged.

Television

149 Television's done wonders for my education, you know. Every time somebody turns it on I go into the other room and read a book.

Toast

150 Isn't technology marvellous? Every morning we used to burn our toast. Now, with modern gadgetry in the kitchen, we can have the burnt toast pop up for us – automatically!

Travel

151 I was at a bazaar. You know how they'll try to sell you just about anything. This chap's crying, 'Genuine skull of Moses.' So I nips over to have a look. But it was a hell of a price, and I told him so.

'Ah,' he said, 'then have this one. It's cheaper because it's smaller. This is the skull of Moses as a child.'

152 A foreigner had gone back to his own country after extensive travel on Britain's railways.

'Trains in Britain are quite unlike those anywhere else,' he told his listeners. 'Why, they have carriages for anything and everything. I have seen carriages not only labelled Smoking, but Reading, Bath and Sandwich.'

Truth

153 The only time a fisherman tells the truth is when he calls another fisherman a liar.

United States of America

154 It was on a sightseeing coach tour of New York that a Welshman turned to his companion, a boastful American, and said, 'And where do you come from?'

'Why, from God's own country,' the American replied.

'Funny,' said the Welshman. 'You don't have a very good Welsh accent.'

155 A father was asking his son what he'd learned at school that day.

'All about George Washington,' answered the boy.

'And what makes him stand out among all the other famous Americans?' asked the father.

And the boy replied, 'He was the one who never told a lie.'

Vicars

156 We're very devout churchgoers, you know. But lately in our parish the vicar's asked for money for the church roof fund, the children's annual outing, the new church hall, new hymn books. We're not so much the flock but the fleeced.

Waiters

157 Oh, are you the waiter who took my order? I was expecting a much older man.

Widows

158 One of Henry's best friends had died, so shortly after the funeral he called on the widow in order to express his sympathy.

'John and I were very good friends,' he told her. 'You know I'd rather like a memento of some kind to remember him by.'

The widow raised her tear-stained eyes and looked at Henry.

'Will *I* do?' she asked.

Words

159 It's odd how some words come to us. I learned the other day that animals derive *their* languages in deceptively simple ways. For instance, do you know why owls look so dejected when it's pouring with rain? No? Well, they're very amorous, you see, and when it's raining heavily all they can do is sit in their trees or barns and wail, 'Too wet to woo, too wet to woo...'

25

Index of Jokes

Reference numbers shown are those of the joke, not the page.